THE LAW OF
FORGIVENESS

THE LAW OF
FORGIVENESS

TAP IN TO THE POSITIVE POWER OF FORGIVENESS—
AND ATTRACT GOOD THINGS TO YOUR LIFE

Connie Domino, MPH, RN

BERKLEY BOOKS, NEW YORK

THE BERKLEY PUBLISHING GROUP
Published by the Penguin Group
Penguin Group (USA) Inc.
375 Hudson Street, New York, New York 10014, USA
Penguin Group (Canada), 90 Eglinton Avenue East, Suite 700, Toronto, Ontario M4P 2Y3, Canada
(a division of Pearson Penguin Canada Inc.)
Penguin Books Ltd., 80 Strand, London WC2R 0RL, England
Penguin Group Ireland, 25 St. Stephen's Green, Dublin 2, Ireland (a division of Penguin Books Ltd.)
Penguin Group (Australia), 250 Camberwell Road, Camberwell, Victoria 3124, Australia
(a division of Pearson Australia Group Pty. Ltd.)
Penguin Books India Pvt. Ltd., 11 Community Centre, Panchsheel Park, New Delhi—110 017, India
Penguin Group (NZ), 67 Apollo Drive, Rosedale, North Shore, 0632, New Zealand
(a division of Pearson New Zealand Ltd.)
Penguin Books (South Africa) (Pty.) Ltd., 24 Sturdee Avenue, Rosebank, Johannesburg 2196,
South Africa

Penguin Books Ltd., Registered Offices: 80 Strand, London WC2R 0RL, England

The publisher does not have any control over and does not assume any responsibility for author or third-party websites or their content.

Scripture taken from the HOLY BIBLE, NEW INTERNATIONAL VERSION®. Copyright © 1973, 1978, 1984 International Bible Society. Used by permission of Zondervan. All rights reserved.

The "NIV" and "New International Version" trademarks are registered in the United States Patent and Trademark Office by International Bible Society. Use of either trademark requires the permission of International Bible Society.

PRINTING HISTORY
Berkley trade paperback edition / November 2009

Library of Congress Cataloging-in-Publication Data

Domino, Connie.
    The law of forgiveness : tap in to the positive power of forgiveness and attract good things
to your life / Connie Domino.
        p.   cm.
    Includes bibliographical references.
    ISBN 978-0-425-22995-8 (alk. paper)
    1. Forgiveness.   I. Title.
    BF637.F67D66 2009
    158.2—dc22

                                                                            2009031220

PRINTED IN THE UNITED STATES OF AMERICA

10 9 8 7 6 5 4 3

I dedicate this book to my husband, Mike, who has been so supportive and helpful in writing this book, and to our beautiful children, Joanna and Matthew, for their love and support. I also dedicate this book to my Law of Attraction and Law of Forgiveness students who have taught me as much about these amazing universal laws as I have them.

CONTENTS

FOREWORD

The book you are about to read will change your life.

In fact, if you asked me to identify the quickest way to change your life, my answer would be just one word: *forgiveness*. Forgiveness is the key to moving beyond your past and unlocking the treasures of the future. It transforms you and moves you into a brand-new world that is beyond your wildest dreams. Love, prosperity, peace . . . it's all there for you. All you have to do is reach out and grab it.

How do I know? Because this is exactly what happened to me when I met Connie Domino.

Simply put . . . forgiveness changed my life.

To properly explain my journey of forgiveness, let me briefly explain where I came from. I was raised in New York City by an upper-middle-class family. Anger, fear, greed and alcoholism were daily visitors in my house, while love and respect were rarely seen. It was an extremely dark childhood and I fled from it as soon as I was old enough. I won't go into what happened, but anyone who grew up in a dysfunctional family can fill in the blanks. Let's just say that it was a very dark world for me.

By my eighteenth birthday, all the garbage that had gone on in my family started to make me angry. However, unlike most people who let their anger come out, I stuffed my anger inside and presented a neutral face to the world so that I could pretend everything was all right. I swallowed my feelings and continued to go on. Not a very healthy thing to do.

By the age of twenty-five, the anger inside me started to affect my posture as my shoulders started to curve and stoop, making me look like an old woman. It was almost as if the weight of the anger was literally wearing me down, which of course it was. It got so bad that when I walked down the street I would look down at my feet, rarely looking anyone in the eye. It was amazing that I didn't bump into things!

By the age of thirty-five, I had so much pent-up anger stored in my body that I was starting to get sick all the time. Every week I had something new—colds, flu, bronchitis, pneumonia—you name it, I seemed to get it. The "dark years" (as I affectionately refer to them now) had worn down my self-esteem to almost nothing, and I became quite adept at dredging up the past and wallowing in it. I looked at the world through negative glasses, and saw it as a hard and cold place. I had been deeply wounded to the very core of my being, and I didn't know how to move past it.

The anger even affected my business, as the company my husband and I were trying to start was struggling to get off the ground. We had clients, of course, but every day was a struggle to survive. By the time I hit my forties, money was tight and bankruptcy was knocking on our door.

It was about this time that I began to understand that the anger was eating me alive. So began my journey of self-discovery, a journey that lasted for the next several years. I learned how to get in touch with my intuition, and then I learned how to listen to it and trust it. I read books, attended workshops and really started to listen to my inner voice/intuition. In 2001, I even wrote a book about it called *God, Is That You?* I learned to trust the guidance that I was being given, and I learned to follow my heart. My journey had begun.

Life got better, our finances started to improve, and I began to understand the past and those dark years of so long ago. I couldn't forgive my family for what they had done, but I understood it and was able to move beyond it. And by following my inner voice, I was able to get our finances straightened out, and our company started to move forward.

What I didn't understand back then was that there was still some anger stuffed deep down inside myself that I consciously didn't know was still there. I was healing, but that little core of hurt was preventing me from reaching my full potential in my business and in my life.

The following year something incredible happened that changed my life forever. It allowed me to finally move beyond the past and into a world of love and peace. Since then, our business has taken off like a brushfire. We never filed that bankruptcy that we'd been considering, and we are now debt-free. And my childhood family is a piece of history that I can calmly look back at (and even write about) with no anger at all. It's as if the hard drive in my brain has been erased and a new program filled with love, respect, peace, integrity and kindness is running in place of the old program. I am filled with an unbelievable amount of love now, and I look at the world positively. The anger that was inside of me for over forty years is gone forever.

What happened?

It was the spring of 2003, and I was at an exposition exhibiting one of my books when my intuition/inner voice nudged me to go over to meet a woman who was talking about the workshops she gave. It was Connie Domino. About a week or so later, Connie taught me about the Law of Forgiveness. It was the last piece I needed in my journey of self-discovery, and I was finally ready for it.

Even though most of Connie's forgiveness students progress more quickly, for me the forgiveness lesson took more than a year to complete because it was like peeling back the layers of an onion. One layer led to another, which led to another, and so on. Every layer brought up a few more memories, causing me to forgive a few more people each time. Eventually, I reached that inner core of anger and the onion was gone, but it sure took a while. Connie encouraged me by saying that persistence pays, because even if it takes some people longer than others, it's so worth it.

After attending Connie's class, I sat down on my bed and decided to start with the easy grudges from my past, leaving the harder ones for last. Why? Mostly because I wasn't ready to forgive my parents right at that moment—that leap was just too huge for me.

So I closed my eyes and a name immediately formed in my mind, which was interesting because I hadn't thought of this person in a very long time. It was an old friend of mine from high school. We had had a falling-out years ago and hadn't spoken to each other since. Looking back, I could easily see what had happened between us and found that I could finally forgive her completely. I immediately (out loud in the empty room) said the forgiveness affirmation that I had learned in Connie's class, and then I went downstairs for a cup of tea.

Two hours later, my friend called me on the phone! I hadn't heard from her in years. After we patched things up, I got curious and asked her why, after all these years, she'd decided to call me today. She said that two hours before (which was the exact time that I was saying my affirmation), an earring that I had given her in high school fell off of her bureau and it made her think about me, so she decided to call.

Unbelievable!

This empowered me to continue with my forgiveness plan, especially as I started to feel a little better. So I kept going and forgave more and more people from my past. It took me quite a few days to do because I only did a few at a time, but soon I had forgiven everyone I could think of. A few weeks later I was even able to forgive myself.

Then an amazing thing happened. I started to feel better physically. I was no longer getting sick, and my head felt clearer somehow. I felt like I had woken up from a long sleep. My posture even got better as I started to stand up straighter.

Then an even more amazing thing happened. The sales from our company started to increase! Absolutely incredible.

Why did my company's sales go up just as I was forgiving people from my past? I couldn't believe that the two were related, and yet they were . . . I was living proof that the Law of Forgiveness works.

As the weeks passed, I found that the more people I forgave, the more my life changed for the better. I began to see the world in a more positive light. People around me started to notice that I looked different and began to ask me if I had changed my hair or lost weight. My skin even looked better!

About six months later, my family decided to revisit a question that had been weighing on our minds: whether to sell or keep a family home that had belonged to my late grandfather. Unfortunately, as is usual in my family, people were fighting over what should be done with it; everyone had a different opinion, and no one could agree on anything. Weeks turned into months, with no end in sight.

One night as I was sitting on my bed watching television, it occurred to me that if I could get my family into one room together, they could finally forgive each other and move on. It had worked so well in my life that I was sure it would help them. I also knew that to sell the house, they would have to get past their anger for each other. Unfortunately this was not logistically possible since most of them had already passed away, and the ones who were still around lived in different parts of the United States. Not to mention the fact that many of them weren't speaking to each other.

So, upon Connie's suggestion, I decided to do it virtually.

Can you imagine your childhood bedroom in your mind right now? Can you see the bed? Can you see the color of the walls? This is what I'm talking about—visualization. So that night, I sat down on my bed and daydreamed. I literally directed a virtual play about what I wanted to happen, and I watched it unfold in my mind.

I imagined that my family members were standing next to one another around a big table. My family had broken into warring factions years ago, but now I envisioned the fighting family units standing with each other. I then imagined that I was at the head of the table and I told them about forgiveness: what it would do for their lives, and how it had changed mine. I "saw" them all in my mind and I spoke out loud to them . . . let's just ignore the fact that I was talking to my empty bedroom!

I then imagined that I turned to each family group and told them to talk to the others to see if they could come to a place of forgiveness. I watched each family group talk, and I smiled when they said the forgiveness affirmation for each other. I imagined that my brother and father spoke to each other and forgave each other. I then imagined that they all said my forgiveness affirmation in unison and I made them hug one another after they did it. It was done.

Of course, I'm pretty sure that they would never do this in real life, but this was my daydream and I could imagine anything that I wanted to, right? Even if it didn't work, at least I felt better about all of it.

The next day the strangest thing happened. After exchanging a few e-mails with my family, I found myself becoming the lead in the family negotiations, which was odd in itself, as I'm the youngest in the family. I took a deep breath and shot off dozens of e-mails to family members, and had the matter peacefully settled in forty-eight hours. The house sold just weeks later, which was really amazing because the family had been "talking" about it for years!

A few months later I was cleaning out our garage and I stumbled across an old box that belonged to my late father. There really wasn't much inside of it, just a few diplomas, some old pictures and a coffee mug. I took the pictures out of the box and idly flipped through them. Then it happened. I came across a wedding picture of my parents, and as I stared at it I saw their lives flash before my eyes. I could see the world they lived in, and the choices they made because of it. I saw the entire generation in an instant and was left with the feeling that they had done the best they could. Tears fell from my face as I forgave my parents instantly, and I said my forgiveness affirmation as I stood there. As I walked back to the kitchen, I felt a weight lift off my shoulders. The weight I'd carried on my shoulders was lighter somehow. Crazy, right? And yet, I undeniably felt the burden lift. I had finally reached that inner core of anger. I was done and finally ready to move forward into a brand-new world.

Forgiveness causes things to move fast, so buckle your seat belt!

It's hard to move forward if you are constantly looking backward. The anger that you are holding on to is a form of energy that gets bottled up inside of you. It becomes twisted and strange, makes you sick, and prevents you from moving forward in your life. Soon the anger is all you can think about, and it becomes your entire focus. You live it, breathe it, dream it and drink it in every day. Sure, you can stuff it down deep inside yourself, but it's still sitting there quietly like a poisonous snake ready to strike at any time. You can even tell yourself that you've forgiven the person, but have you really? Do you still feel angry at the mention of the person's name?

Once you forgive someone, the energy is released and everything begins to flow in the proper direction. It's like a river that has a dam on it. Remove the dam and the water begins to flow again. Fish, ducks, turtles and geese return.

That's forgiveness.

After I forgave everyone, my life began to flow again and I am now in a place that is filled with peace, prosperity and love. I can look back at my past, and now I can see the love that was there. I can even see my lighthouses—the people who showed me the way out. They guided me through the storms of life and provided a light for me to follow out of the darkness. They showed me how to negotiate the rocks and navigate through the fog and severe storms that came along in my life. My lighthouses are the people I remember now. In fact, I really can't remember those dark days very well any longer. It's as if they've been erased from my mind and are now gone completely.

This was confirmed recently when my two sons asked me about my childhood, and I couldn't remember a lot of it. Stunned, I tried harder to come up with something to tell them and in the end managed to remember a few funny stories. What makes this so incredible is that only a few years ago I could recount all sorts of things. Today it's gone completely and has been replaced by hazy, happy memories. It's as if the negativity has been erased from my hard drive and replaced with positive memories. Of course I can dredge things up if I really think about it, but I have no desire to do so anymore. The past has been healed and I have moved on.

When did I know that I was finally through it all and on the other side? When did I know that I had finally forgiven them all?

It was the day when I realized that my family no longer had the kind of power over me that I once allowed them to have. They no longer caused an emotional reaction in me when I thought of them. I could finally look at them with peace and understanding, and knew the past no longer mattered to me. It was over. That's when I knew that I had finally moved on.

Forgiveness is a journey. I am constantly surprised at the doors that have opened for me because of it. People that I thought were gone for good have returned, and situations that I thought were impossible to rectify have been miraculously turned around. Forgiveness is transforming and offers you a new perspective and a fresh start. It's a journey that will continue for the rest of my life.

Today my world is filled with love and prosperity. I look at the world in a positive way and I'm finally at peace. Now it's my turn to pass it forward to others who might be living where I was. My life's work is to be a lighthouse—to guide people safely to their harbors so that they can live a life of peace, love and prosperity.

Thank you, Connie. Thank you for being one of my lighthouses. Thank you for providing a light to guide us all out of the darkness.

Katharine C. Giovanni

Author, Speaker, Consultant, International Concierge Training Expert, and author of the new book Going Above and Beyond: How to Think and Act Like a Concierge

www.triangleconcierge.com and www.katharinegiovanni.com

INTRODUCTION

In 2001, I began teaching workshops on the Law of Attraction. Participants who had been working on their dreams and goals for many years came and were able to meet those goals in several weeks once they began practicing the Law of Attraction. I was amazed and awed by this spiritual and social law. In 2004, I wrote *Develop Irresistible Attraction* describing how to use the Law of Attraction. And after the DVD *The Secret* brought the Law of Attraction to a worldwide audience at the beginning of 2007, I was able to substantially increase the number of people I could reach who wanted to learn how to apply this law in their own lives.

The Law of Attraction is a universal law open to use by anyone who understands it. Just like the law of gravity, it is predictable and unchanging. While the law of gravity is a physical law that has influence over our physical existence, the Law of Attraction is a *spiritual* or *social* law. Both spiritual and physical laws can be considered *natural* and both have a predictable set of properties that can be used to affect the physical or material world. We have studied the Law of Gravity and other physical laws for years and understand them well, but we are just beginning to discover and seriously study the spiritual, or social, laws of the universe. So, how does the Law of Attraction affect you personally? The Law of Attraction teaches us that:

- All that we are experiencing in our lives, we have attracted (both the good and bad) by our thoughts, feelings, prayers, actions, inactions, and soul-level decisions.

- We can change our circumstances by changing the way we think (and *feel*), what we believe, what we say to ourselves (our self-talk) and the actions we take.

- The energy needed to make our dreams come true is already available, and is waiting for our thoughts and beliefs to manifest it into the material world.

- Love is the energy, and belief is the vehicle for manifestation. There is nothing in existence stronger than love and belief.

We can literally create our reality, create the life we want and manifest our desires, goals and dreams by using the Law of Attraction.

In 2002, after providing several Law of Attraction workshops, I noticed that teaching participants about this powerful spiritual law was not enough. Some people in my workshops were not manifesting as quickly as others, even though they were following the same steps. It became apparent that many people were blocking their dreams and goals from manifesting due to their anger, resentment and lack of forgiveness. I added the Law of Forgiveness to my workshop when I noticed that my divorced participants were not manifesting their goals as quickly as those who were never married, or who had never been divorced. The divorced people were full of anger and resentment. You could even hear it in their voices when they spoke. It was also apparent that it wasn't only those who were divorced, but others who were angry with family, friends or coworkers, who were slow to manifest. It became clear to me that these people needed to release their anger in order to open themselves to the prosperity that the universe could give them. Hence I began teaching the Law of Forgiveness. Little did I know that I was unleashing the most powerful strategy for personal success I had ever witnessed. While I teach a number of strategies to activate the Law of Attraction, I had no idea that the Law of Forgiveness would help people manifest their goals faster and change their lives more profoundly than anything I had ever seen. The stories started pouring in about how, time after time, the Law of Forgiveness had profoundly affected my readers and workshop participants. Not only were they meeting goals and dreams, but their lives were healed in ways they had never imagined. After watching the amazing transformation over and over again, I began to see that the Law of Forgiveness could not only change the lives of individuals, but had the potential to—literally—change the world. It was then that I was moved to write a book solely dedicated to this powerful law.

This book contains all of the information that you will need to use the amazing Law of Forgiveness in your own life. When you do, in the words of Henry David Thoreau, you will ". . . pass an invisible boundary, new universal and more liberal laws will begin to establish themselves. . . [and you will] live with the license of a higher order of beings."

How This Book Is Different from Other Books on Forgiveness

Are you saying to yourself, "Not another book on forgiveness? What could Connie possibly teach me that I haven't already heard over and over again?" Well, hold on, because I will teach you a simple, easy-to-use technique that can quickly change your life forever.

In my review of books on forgiveness, I found that they do a good job of teaching *what* forgiveness is about. Some books even go into detail, teaching you concrete steps and extensive exercises you can use to forgive. They all concentrate on how forgiveness will make you feel better mentally, emotionally, socially—even physically. However, not one book I found taught a simple technique for forgiving that will assist you to make your dreams and goals come true . . . quickly. None of the books even equated forgiveness with meeting dreams and goals. Yes, forgiveness actually helps you get where you desire to go, and it's the fast-track way to get there. If you've been struggling to achieve happiness and success, it may interest you to know that lack of forgiveness may be the largest barrier in your life— it could be blocking dreams and goals in every area of your life from manifesting.

The technique I will be sharing with you does not involve lengthy, time-consuming exercises. It's not a "thirty days to this" or "ninety days to that" approach. The forgiveness technique begins to work immediately when you sincerely implement it. I have seen people manifest goals within five minutes! Some manifestations take a little longer—from a few hours, to perhaps a week after fully incorporating the forgiveness technique. There are also individuals who take even longer to fully work through forgiveness, due to the nature of their own situations.

This technique can be done in the privacy of your home. You don't have to contact anyone and there is no need for special equipment, skills, prior knowledge or training. It is remarkable in its simplicity, and I am convinced that is why we have missed it all these years. Believe it or not, you don't have to crawl over broken glass and show scars, or go through any other torturous process in order to learn to forgive and experience the amazing results that follow. I will teach you *how* to forgive and, just as important, how to know when you have forgiven.

What Is the Law of Forgiveness?

It may sound unusual to be referring to forgiveness as a law, but that's exactly what it is. Forgiveness is a spiritual or social law that, when enacted, can affect the material world. Just like the physical Law of Gravity, it is universal and unchanging. It has a set of properties you can use again and again with positive results. Energy moves when forgiveness is enacted by someone who is sincere about forgiving.

Like the Law of Attraction, we are just beginning to learn about all the possibilities inherent in forgiveness. As stated previously, predictable and unchanging laws govern our universe and our existence. When we understand these laws and are in alignment with them, our lives run more smoothly, more positively, and we can accomplish much more in a shorter period of time. Some laws, such as the Law of Gravity, we understand well and are able to use to benefit our everyday existence. We are just beginning to understand other laws, such as the Law of Attraction and the Law of Forgiveness. Like the Law of Gravity, once we learn about these laws, we can incorporate them into our daily lives, make practical application of them, and experience amazing results.

If we allow these natural laws to guide and teach us, we will learn great wisdom. The late psychologist and minister Dan Custer wrote in *The Miracle of Mind Power*:

> Nature is the great giver and great forgiver. Should you cut your hand with a sharp knife, the forces of nature set about immediately to repair the damage. It was a mistake to cut your hand, but nature does not withhold the repairing of the wound. Nature immediately forgives and starts at once to make repairs . . . Nature even repairs the ravages of the battlefield by covering it with grass and flowers. Nature brings us back into harmony, back to happiness and peace if we do our part, so to forgive is natural.

Semantics

There are a number of words and phrases people use to refer to forgiveness: *released, let go of, pardoned*. But like the Law of Gravity, the Law of Forgiveness is natural, universal, consistent and unchanging. Therefore, it does not matter what words we use; its properties will remain the same. To illustrate this point, consider the Law of Gravity. Gravity doesn't care whether you're a Christian, Hindu, Muslim, Jew, atheist, Buddhist or something else altogether—gravity is a constant force and it reacts in the same manner no matter who you are or what you believe. If a person steps off the top of a twenty-one-story building, the Law of Gravity is predictable in what will happen next, regardless of that person's belief system. The Law of Forgiveness is the same. Regardless of your spiritual belief system, if you use the Law of Forgiveness, it will work for you.

Nurse researcher Ann Gentry and her colleagues studied the origin of the word *forgiveness*. They discovered that the origin of the *for* in forgiveness derives from the Middle English and Anglo-Saxon word *fore,* which can mean *away*. The origin of the word *give* derives from the Middle English word *geve*, which developed from the Old Norse word *gefa*, meaning to turn something over to someone else. Many people believe when they forgive they are giving a *gift* of pardon to the person who offended them. However, when they use the Law of Forgiveness and have given away or let go of their anger and resentment, they find that, to their surprise, the *gift* becomes theirs in the form of more peace, happiness and well-being—and best of all, in meeting their goals and dreams.

It is important that the words you choose to use when you enact the Law of Forgiveness resonate with you. Some people have asked me if they can use the word *release* instead of forgive. When you practice forgiveness, you are *releasing* the past to enjoy a more positive future. This doesn't mean you're condoning or forgetting the transgression, but are, instead, releasing its hold on your life. So, if the word *release* works better for you, it's fine to use it.

If I use any words when discussing the Law of Forgiveness that are not words you normally use, just change them to words that work for you. I will use the words *prayer*, *thoughts* and *meditation* interchangeably. You may choose the one that best fits your philosophy and practice. I was raised in the Christian tradition; therefore, I will be using some examples from my own faith experience. You may wish to think of examples from your own faith tradition, philosophy or experience. It's also fine if you have no faith preference or tradition, the Law of Forgiveness will work for you.

You will see in the next section, that all the world's most predominent religions teach about the importance of forgiveness. In addition, they all teach some form of the Golden Rule. When compared, we have much more in common with people of differing faiths than many of us imagined. The main thing is to not get caught up in semantics or you will miss one of the most exciting laws I have ever studied for manifesting your goals and dreams, healing your life and making the world a better place.

Forgiveness in World Religions

We hear about the importance of forgiveness constantly, from our spiritual and religious leaders. Every major world religion teaches that forgiveness is necessary and important. Forgiveness is truly a universally accepted principle and provides common ground for love, acceptance, harmony and true happiness. The Dalai Lama, the spiritual and temporal leader of Tibet, believes that happiness is a natural part of our very existence. In his book *The Art of Happiness* the Dalai Lama says, "The very purpose of our life is to seek happiness. That is clear. Whether one believes in religion or not, whether one believes in this religion or that religion, we are all seeking something better in life. So I think, the very motion of our life is toward happiness." Most spiritual and religious leaders will agree that forgiveness of oneself and others is one way to clear the mind, heart and soul and may result in a feeling of increased peace and happiness.

Our religions—with their millions and millions of followers— can play a major role in assisting people to find peace within themselves and with others. It would be a great example and very helpful if religious leaders could forgive and make peace with one another. In a world where there has been so much conflict down through the ages over our differing religious beliefs, it is worth discussing forgiveness within this context. Interestingly, when comparing religions it becomes obvious that forgiveness is one of the *many* teachings they have in common.

Buddhism

Buddhism teaches that believers should essentially practice prevention—the idea being that acting in lovingkindness, compassion and sympathetic joy will enable followers to avoid developing resentments that would necessitate forgiveness. Buddhism recognizes the damage that anger and resentment can have on the mind and mental well-being. Those practicing Buddhism are encouraged to release their resentments through meditation in order to prevent the continuing cycle of suffering that can result.

Christianity

Christianity teaches that forgiveness originates with God. Christian believers are taught they are to forgive others as God has forgiven them. There are a variety of denominations within Christianity, each with a slightly differing viewpoint. Most Christian denominations believe that God's ultimate forgiveness for the sins or wrongful actions of humanity comes through accepting the blood of Jesus as the ultimate sacrifice and substitute for his justice. They are taught to pray and ask God for forgiveness for their sins. On the other hand, there are some Christians who believe that our sense of separateness from God is actually an illusion that leads to guilt and fear. They believe we can release this sense of guilt and fear through the practice of forgiveness. In forgiving others, we learn to forgive ourselves and thus our illusions of separateness can be healed. The Apostle Paul, who played a major role in establishing Christianity, said, "Forgive as the Lord forgave you."

◼ Hinduism

Those practicing Hinduism believe that forgiveness contains great power in and of itself. The Hindu leader Vidura said,

> Forgiveness subdues (all) in this world; what is there that forgiveness cannot achieve? What can a wicked person do unto him who carries the sabre of forgiveness in his hand? Fire falling on the grassless ground is extinguished of itself. And the unforgiving individual defiles himself with many enormities. Righteousness is the one highest good; and forgiveness is the one supreme peace; knowledge is the one supreme contentment; and benevolence, one sole happiness. (From *Mahabharata,* Udyoga Parva Section XXXIII, Translated by Sri Kisari Mohan Ganguli.)

Hindus also believe in asking the Lord to forgive them. One of their temple ceremony invocations begins with asking the Lord to forgive sins due to their human limitations.

◼ Islam

Those practicing Islam believe that followers should forgive each other, and they can also be forgiven by Allah (*God* in Arabic). They believe the source of forgiveness is determined by the wrong being committed. If the wrong needs divine forgiveness from Allah, the person asking should be repentant. If one human is forgiving another, it is important to both forgive and be forgiven.

To receive forgiveness from Allah, in addition to asking for forgiveness, the believer must recognize and admit the wrongdoing before Allah, and make a commitment to not repeat the offense. If another person is involved, in addition to these three requirements, the believer must also ask for pardon from the offended person and make amends within reason. As the Qur'an says, "Keep to forgiveness, and enjoin kindness." (7:199–200.)

Judaism

In Judaism, believers seek forgiveness from God and people. However, they can only seek forgiveness from God for wrongs that have been committed against God. When they have wronged another person, they must seek forgiveness from that individual. If the person seeking forgiveness is sincere and honest in their apology, the person wronged is required by Judaism to grant forgiveness. If the offender does not apologize, the person who is wronged isn't religiously required to forgive them unless they choose to. The Torah reads, "When asked by an offender for forgiveness, one should forgive with a sincere mind and a willing spirit . . . forgiveness is natural to the seed of Israel" (Mishneh Torah, *Teshuvah* 2:10).

Yom Kippur is probably the most important day in the Jewish faith—it's the official Day of Atonement. During this day, Jews fast, pray and ask for God's forgiveness for any wrongs they have committed against God during the prior year. Just before Yom Kippur, Jews can right any wrong they have committed against another person during the prior year by asking their forgiveness, if they haven't already done so.

Because so many people are familiar with the topic of forgiveness through their faith tradition, they are very open to trying the forgiveness technique and then teaching it to others.

Some people have asked me if they can forgive through their higher power. For example, they may say, "Through the grace of

🪷 The Golden Rule

In addition to encouraging forgiveness, every religion teaches some form of the Golden Rule. If I were asked to distill the essence of all religions into one sentence, it would be: Love God/higher power, love yourself, forgive others and forgive yourself, be kind to others and yourself, treat others as you would like to be treated. If everyone in the world abided by this simple admonition, what a lovely place the world would be.

In reviewing this list which contains the Golden Rule defined by religions the world over, it becomes obvious that we have much more in common with each other than we have differences. If we embraced this simple rule taught the world over, what a difference it would make!

Baha'l Faith "Ascribe not to any soul that which thou wouldst not have ascribed to thee, and say not that which thou doest not... And if thine eyes be turned towards justice, choose thou for thy neighbor that which thou choosest for thyself."

Buddhism "Hurt not others in ways that you yourself would find hurtful."

Udana-Varga 5:18

Confucianism "Tse-kung asked, 'Is there one word that can serve as a principle of conduct for your life?' Confucius replied, 'It is the word *shu*—reciprocity. Do not impose on others what you yourself do not desire."

Doctrine of the Mean 13.3

God, I forgive you," or something similar. I think that's fine as long as you are still sincerely forgiving the person. The major religions mentioned above speak of the importance of both God's forgiveness of us and our forgiveness of each other. In other words, it's fine if you wish to forgive through God, as long as you understand that you are still personally and sincerely forgiving the person(s) who wronged you.

Christianity "Therefore all things whatsoever ye would that men should do to you, do ye even so to them: for this is the law and the prophets."

Matthew 7:12 (KJV)

Islam "None of you [truly] believes until he wishes for his brother what he wishes for himself."

Number 13 of Imam "Al-Nawawi's Forty Hadiths"

Judaism "What is hateful to you, do not do to your fellow man. This is the Law: all the rest is commentary."

Talmud, Shabbat 31a

Native Spirituality "All things are our relatives; what we do to everything, we do to ourselves. All is really One."

Black Elk

Taoism "Regard your neighbor's gain as your own gain, and your neighbor's loss as your own loss."

Tai Shang Kan Ying P'ien

Unitarianism "We affirm and promote respect for the interdependent web of all existence of which we are a part."

Forgive Your Enemies

There are stories from every faith tradition about the importance of forgiving those who have wronged you. In this section, I will use an example I am familiar with from Christianity. You are encouraged to find examples in your belief system, faith, practice or philosophy. In the Christian tradition, Jesus' message was to "Love your enemies, and forgive those who persecute you." According to the New Testament, when Jesus was crucified, he forgave his persecutors: "Father, forgive them, for they know not what they are doing." When Jesus forgave his enemies and taught us to do the same, he wasn't just talking about a nice spiritual thing to do for others. He was trying to convey the idea that there is actual metaphysical power in the act of forgiveness. Jesus taught us through his words and actions, when we forgive we are in reality blocking negative energy (some refer to as evil) and disarming the enemy. Now, that's power!

You may need to read those last two sentences several times, as it may take a minute or two for you to wrap your head around this concept, because in our society, we have not been taught to equate the word "forgiveness" with the word "power." In fact it is unfortunate that we have been taught to equate the word "forgiveness" with the words, "condoning, giving in, and weak surrender." However, there are many stories told down through the ages and into the present demonstrating the true nature of forgiveness as a strategy of great power. So many stories have been told about people who, under frightening circumstances, were able to get into that space of love, acceptance and forgiveness toward their assailant just as they were about to be assaulted, robbed and possibly even killed. They were all surprised when their would-be-attackers literally turned and walked or ran away.

In March 2005, this very principle was demonstrated by Ashley Smith from Atlanta, Georgia, while she was held hostage by Brian Nichols, who had just killed a judge and three other people. During this frightening ordeal, she managed to gain the trust of Nichols. In later interviews she said she just talked to him about love of family and the importance of faith. "I basically just talked to him and tried to gain his trust. I wanted to leave to go see my daughter. That was really important. I didn't want him to hurt anybody else." In addition, she engaged him in a discussion about life's purpose, and each person's gifts and talents. She simply spoke with him and expressed love and understanding. While frightened for her life, Ashley was still able to get in a space of empathy, understanding and forgiveness.

The next morning, Brian allowed Ashley to leave freely to visit her daughter, knowing she could contact the police. Ashley did call 9-1-1, and even with several loaded guns in his possession, Brian offered no resistance as he left with authorities.

Through the authentic power of love and forgiveness, Ashley (as many others before her) was able to disarm her attacker. I believe this is because the energetic vibration level emitted by Ashley increased so much when she brought forth true love and empathy that, in response, the would-be assailant could not resist the energy change and had no choice but to put down his weapons. Can you now see that forgiveness is an actual strategy or tactic so powerful, so full of energy, that it can not only change the lives of individuals, but literally change the world if applied on a large scale?

How do we learn to vibrate at that level—high enough to forgive people who hurt us, or want to hurt us? For years we have been admonished to forgive, but were never taught how to do so; this book is about just that—the skill behind the goal.

In Lynn Grabhorn's excellent book *Excuse Me Your Life Is Waiting,* she details and clarifies how our "feelings" determine how we vibrate, and our vibratory level determines what we are experiencing in our lives. We are all made of energy, as is everything else. Not only does energy travel in waves, but scientists have now determined that energy also "vibrates." Lynn clearly explains that we are vibrating "magnets" of the universe. Positive feelings cause us to vibrate at a higher level, and vibrating high feels good because it is our natural spiritual state. Negative feelings make us vibrate low, which may make us feel bad or numb, or can even cause us to feel nothing because we may be so accustomed to vibrating low. As energetic magnets, we will attract people, circumstances or things according to where we are vibrating. So, if you have had what seems like a "run of bad luck," look where you're vibrating, as like attracts like.

For many people, rage and resentment are causing them to vibrate very low and they are blocking much of the energy they need to manifest their desired goals. As previously mentioned, this is especially true for people who were either divorced or going through a divorce. They had a lot of anger and lack of forgiveness toward their ex-spouse. Because of bitterness about alimony, child support and who got the speed boat, many participants could not free the energy they needed to manifest their dreams and goals until they had fully invoked the Law of Forgiveness. When they unleashed all the energy they had tied up in not forgiving, and in resentment and hurt, they began reaching their goals immediately. This also applies to people who come to my workshops carrying anger at bosses who fired them unfairly, parents who abused or neglected them, teenagers who abused their trust, or any number of other reasons—anything that makes one human get angry at another. By learning and applying the Law of Forgiveness, surges of energy become available to you, right here and now. Your goals rush into the vacuum left by your anger.

Everything is composed of energy, and that energy travels in waves. Scientists have discovered that energy is neither created nor destroyed, but changes from one state to another (this is known in physics as the First Law of Thermodynamics). Therefore, energy is malleable. For the purpose of our discussion, you can think of energy as modeling clay. In that sense, the energy stuff of the universe can be fashioned by our creative process to make our dreams come true. When we are angry, resentful and unforgiving, these emotions become energy dams preventing the energy we need to meet desired goals and dreams. When we forgive and release anger and resentment, the dams are released and the energy that has been blocked is now made available to us to manifest our goals and dreams.

My Personal Journey in Understanding Forgiveness

I first learned about forgiveness from my faith tradition. I can remember, as a child, hearing our minister talk about the importance of forgiveness, but I would think of my current hurts and grievances and wonder how to forgive. Is it enough to just say, "I forgive you?" Or, do you have to feel it and mean it, too, for it to work? Do you have to approach the person and let them know you have forgiven them? Oftentimes, I would think I had forgiven someone, but when old feelings of hurt or anger arose, I would wonder whether I honestly had. In 1988, I had a life-changing opportunity to learn from people who had lived through war on their land and had experienced transformation through forgiveness. My adventure began when I, along with my husband, Mike, and three other chaperones from the church we attended, accompanied ten teenaged boys to Coventry, England. Our church had sent a youth group to Coventry about every three years since the 1970s. During a week of study and work, the youths learn about the Community of the Cross of Nails (CCN) that was begun there after the bombing of St. Michael's Cathedral by the German Luftwaffe during World War II. Our faith community felt it was important that young people study the devastation that is wrought by war, and how it can be prevented so that peace and reconciliation can be achieved.

Most of Coventry, England, was destroyed by fire bombs on November 14, 1940. The people of Coventry that we had the opportunity to visit with had been children during this time. They explained what they had experienced, and it was clear that it was still real and vivid in their memories. I expected those who lived through World War II in this country to be profoundly affected, but was a little surprised how every generation afterward was affected as well. Regardless of age, when they talked of the war, it was as if it had happened yesterday. It was still fresh in their minds. Keep in mind that the entire country of England is no bigger than many of the states in America, and much of it was bombed during World War II. As you can imagine, the entire country felt the devastation of the Coventry attack. The British military retaliated for the Coventry bombing by attacking Dresden, Germany, where historians estimate between 24,000 and 40,000 people were killed.

Standing in the ruins of the ancient cathedral, I was impressed by stories of the courage and conviction of Dick Howard, who was the Provost of St. Michael's at the time of the bombing. Instead of concentrating on feelings of bitterness, revenge, hatred and fear, he directed the cathedral's ministry toward forgiveness and reconciliation. After the bombing, the cathedral's stonemason found that two charred beams had fallen in the sign of a cross. He set the cross up in the ruins, and it was later placed on an altar with the words FATHER FORGIVE inscribed beneath.

Because of the decision of a brave clergyman, the Community of the Cross of Nails ministry and the International Centre for Reconciliation arose from the ashes. These organizations have networks and centers around the world providing spiritual and practical solutions in areas of conflict. They work with people of all nationalities and religions in areas such as Northern Ireland, Israel and Palestine, Bosnia and Serbia, Africa, and Iraq. The name, Community of the Cross of Nails, comes from another cross made from the debris found at Coventry after the bombing: This one was fashioned from three of the cathedral's medieval nails by a local priest, the Reverend Arthur Wales. What astonished our group was learning that after the war, young people from Germany and England, who were once bitter enemies, worked together with others to build both a new hospital in Dresden and a new cathedral beside the ruins in Coventry. The Cross of Nails has become the symbol of Coventry's international ministry of peace and reconciliation.

I thought I knew a great deal about forgiveness and reconciliation from my years as an active member of the CCN, serving on both my church committee and the national board, but it was through my own personal and career development that I was able to learn the most important life lessons about forgiveness.

A New Lesson About the Power of Forgiveness

I began my career as a registered nurse. After working for a short time, I made two observations:

- The first observation was that in America, we offer the best emergency or "rescue" medicine in the world. This means if you're having a heart attack, or if you have an accident, or develop pneumonia, or need an appendectomy, or if you're experiencing any acute illness that may end your life quickly, America is a very good place to be.

- The second observation was that Western medicine does not work well for preventing chronic illness. The role that microbes may play in chronic illness has been largely ignored. In addition, Western medicine doesn't pay adequate attention to the fact that many of the chronic diseases causing human misery and suffering may be prevented with lifestyle modifications. For example, avoiding tobacco products and preventing obesity are two health goals that would make a huge impact in preventing certain chronic illnesses. I also came to the realization that these lifestyle diseases can also be impacted by a person's ability to cope with emotional and social stressors.

While Americans are some of the most prosperous people in the world, we have a large population of what I call the "worried well." These are people who enjoy basic physical health, but they're experiencing a constant level of unhappiness, stress and frustration. They don't feel like they're meeting their goals and dreams, they don't feel that their lives are in line with their true purpose, and they are pretty sure they aren't living up to their potential. The stress of this has a negative impact on their physical health.

After working for a few years in hospitals in which the main objective seemed to be to treat bad things *after* they had already happened, I decided to make a career change, and so I earned a master's degree in public health education. I felt I could have a positive impact on more people if I taught them how to promote and protect their health. I was especially interested in working with the "worried well"—assisting them to find their life's purpose and meet their dreams and goals.

True to my decision, through my career as a health educator, I was reaching far more people, and was assisting them in improving their health and well-being. By using a positive prevention approach that concentrated on a person's strengths, talents and abilities, instead of a negative approach that concentrated on the treatment of ailments that were already in place, I was able to help large numbers of people define and reach their own health and wellness goals.

As a health and nursing educator, I taught almost every health promotion topic to every age group: heart health, physical fitness, nutrition, women's health, adolescent health, sexual health, emotional health, stress management, healthy relationships—you name it, I taught it. Agencies and organizations sought my assistance with health promotion grant-writing, program development, implementation and evaluation. I received great reviews on my programs and workshops, and wonderful feedback from many satisfied customers, but I wasn't satisfied. I was always looking for that one workshop that would allow people to walk away with positive tools that would change their lives quickly and forever. After many years of trying, I finally hit on that workshop in 2001. It even surprised me because when I began teaching the workshop, I had no idea of the great impact it would have on people's lives.

In September of 2001, I began teaching a workshop on goal setting for a group of spiritually minded people. I called my workshop Develop Irresistible Attraction and based it on the Law of Attraction. The workshop teaches us that we *attract* situations into our lives by our feelings, thoughts, prayers, actions, inactions and soul-level decisions. In other words, we play a very large role in creating our own reality.

I felt this law of the universe best explained why some people seemed to meet their goals easily and effortlessly while others felt they were always struggling and never quite seemed to achieve what they truly desired. I had studied the positive attitude movement for years and had always wondered why positive thinking and positive techniques worked for some, but not for others. In 2001, with this workshop, I finally discovered the secret to manifesting goals and dreams quickly. I figured out how some people manifest easily. Using these discoveries, I developed a technique for writing goals in a specific manner that brings the conscious and subconscious mind into alignment. I taught people to use a specific type of positive affirmation, stated as a goal, as a way to achieve their desires and dreams.

I also taught participants to examine their self-talk, and to recognize how it had evolved from childhood. I asked them to share any negative self-talk they had in regard to their goals, especially since these negative thoughts and feelings could block their goals from manifesting. I taught them a technique for removing the blocks and barriers. When workshop participants followed my technique, some were able to manifest goals they had been working on for years—and some did it in two weeks. I was completely amazed.

What I discovered, through many years of studying popular self-help, positive spiritual and mental attitude books is that although they covered many of the principles and laws that I cover in my workshops and in my first book, *Law of Attraction: Develop Irresistible Attraction*, they do not place them in a simple, practical formula within a context (the popular framework of goal setting) that people were familiar with and accustomed to using.

I also found that almost all of the goal-setting books ever written would instruct readers to set their goals, but would never ask readers how they "felt" about the goals they set. I discovered that a person's underlying thoughts and feelings about the goals they set, or the vehicle through which they were choosing to meet their goals (if those feelings were negative) could act as "energy blocks" or "psychological blocks" to keep the goal from manifesting. I found that people didn't always recognize their underlying feelings and thoughts about a desired goal. I soon discovered a quick way to assist people in recognizing these underlying feelings and thoughts was to assist them with examining their self-talk and how it evolved from childhood.

When I combined all these discoveries together, I produced a simple five-step formula detailed in *Law of Attraction: Develop Irresistible Attraction* that assists people to become extremely clear about their desired goals. In addition, this formula assists them, through understanding their self-talk, *to identify*, and through the process of positive affirmations, *to remove* any underlying negative thoughts and feelings about their goals. I taught them that lack of forgiveness can be one of the largest blocks or barriers. When energetic or psychological blocks around a desired goal are removed, the conscious mind is brought into alignment with the subconscious mind, and the goal manifests very quickly. My first workshop was scheduled to meet for two hours once a week for a total of four weeks. Two weeks after this workshop began, the World Trade Center was attacked. Eighty percent of my class did not return the third week, as the whole world was in shock. However, the participants who did return had already met the goals they had been working on for several years in just two weeks, or four hours of instruction. They were so excited about their quick manifestations, they couldn't wait to share them and find out how to make other dreams come true.

One woman who returned had been actively trying to get a date for a year and a half without success. She said she was seventy pounds overweight. She also said that she had experienced some miserable past relationships, and she felt that all men were—to use her expression—jerks. She blamed her current problems with men on her bad childhood and the fact that she was overweight. However, she was willing to try the technique I taught because she was in her thirties and felt that her "biological clock" was ticking. She felt she was ready to marry and have children. After only two weeks in the class (just four hours of instruction), she reported that four different men had called in the past week and asked her for a date. Four dates in one week! I was astonished! I know that in all the years that I was single, I had never had four different men ask me for a date in the same week. She had many dates after that. It took her a year to fully work through her issues around marriage and forgive her past, but when she did, she found a nice man to marry and they now have two beautiful children.

In January of 2002, Janelle attended my workshop. She was the first Law of Attraction workshop participant who desired to manifest an altruistic goal. She wanted to manifest a brand-new building for a charter school. She was a member of the charter school's volunteer board; their current building was in disrepair. She listed several difficulties that were standing in the way of obtaining a new building for the school: the school's lack of money, the fact that her board didn't support the idea, the reality that the economy wasn't strong and that funding agencies do not typically pay for building projects. I had just begun teaching the Law of Attraction workshops at that time, and thought to myself that she was probably right. I had worked for non-profit agencies for years and knew how difficult it was to raise money for a new building. This enormous undertaking usually involves a major capital campaign and may take half a decade to raise enough funds. Thank goodness I didn't say anything about my past experience or beliefs!

Janelle agreed to faithfully use the technique I had taught. She completed the four-week, eight-hour workshop in January, and only eight months later, in August, contacted me. She said, "We have a brand-new building, built from the ground up. School is beginning and we're having an opening ceremony today." I was absolutely astonished that this woman could manifest an actual brick-and-mortar building from the ground up in only eight months! I had worked in the not-for-profit sector for years and knew the effort involved in fund-raising to even meet the annual budget, but to build a new building? All I could say was "Wow!"

At this point, I knew I was on to something big, something VERY BIG! I didn't know quite what I had my hands on, but I knew it was important, powerful and remarkable and I wanted to bring this knowledge to the world. I repeated the workshop and found again that participants could meet their goals very quickly by using the technique I was teaching, some in as little as two weeks.

As previously mentioned, I noticed that some people (especially the participants who had experienced divorce) were emotionally blocking their goals from manifesting, because of their anger and lack of forgiveness. It suddenly occurred to me that the process of personal forgiveness had a significant role, even in a workshop on goal setting.

To address this need, I developed guidelines and an affirmation that participants could state, to make forgiveness real for them. I found that, after using this affirmation even the participants who had been blocking their goals due to their anger were suddenly able to manifest their goals quickly. They exhibited the same progress that others in the workshop were making. In fact, the results experienced by many of the previously "reluctant forgivers" were no less than miraculous. The act of forgiving had positively affected every area of their lives.

After working on forgiveness, some participants received money from people or sources that they hadn't heard from in years. For those in business, results included more customers, profits and general prosperity. Relationships improved, sometimes dramatically, and severely broken relationships were healed. Participants said that individuals they had forgiven in the privacy of their own home would call or e-mail them right out of the blue.

I soon discovered that the Law of Forgiveness is the most powerful technique that I teach. The Law of Forgiveness actually activates the Law of Attraction. The Law of Forgiveness is not the Law of Attraction; in fact, in many ways, I have found it to be a much more powerful law. It works faster and more profoundly to assist people in meeting their dreams and goals, compared to anything I have ever seen.

The stories kept coming as more and more people discovered the positive benefits of forgiveness. I began hearing from people all over the world who were interested in learning *how* to forgive.

Some people told me that they had spent tens of thousands of dollars over the years purchasing books, tapes, CDs, DVDs, hiring life/business coaches and attending positive mental attitude, motivational, goal-setting and business-building workshops. However, they had very little to show for their investments as they had never received a clear plan for manifesting their goals, until they met me. After reading my book and attending just one coaching session, Jeremy wrote:

Thank you so much for helping me learn, grow, manifest and create more in my life at a very rapid pace. I have spent years attending personal development and business success programs. I have read many books and spent literally tens of thousands of dollars attending workshops. However, with your incredible book, and one fantastic personal coaching session, I was able to meet two of my three goals in two weeks. These are goals I have been working on for some time. I definitely believe it was the forgiveness technique you taught me that made the biggest difference. I met a goal for a romantic relationship and another personal goal of improving a family relationship. Now, my third goal of significantly increasing my income is also coming true, and I feel euphoric. I have shared your book with so many of my peers, family and associates all over the world, and now they are manifesting, too. I look forward to supporting your work in the future because I know the universe we live in has no limits, and so many people are going to be helped by what you do.

Ever so grateful,
Jeremy

By 2005, people were e-mailing me from all over the world, sharing their manifestation stories. Time after time, they mentioned how the Law of Forgiveness had affected them more profoundly than anything else they had ever used to meet their goals. My readers and clients affectionately began calling me "The Forgiveness Lady." It was at their suggestion that I wrote this book.

Enacting or Invoking Forgiveness

In this chapter you will learn the guidelines for forgiveness and a simple affirmation you can complete in the privacy of your own home to enact or invoke this powerful law. I will refer to this process as the Forgiveness Affiramtion Technique. In addition, I have included just a few of the many stories from readers and workshop participants about the great energy shifts and results they have experienced while utilizing the Law of Forgiveness. Keep in mind that not one of these people contacted the person(s) they were forgiving. They said their affirmation in the privacy of their own home.

Guidelines for Forgiveness

Forgiveness 101

WHO SHOULD I FORGIVE?
You should forgive everyone you can remember, *living or deceased*, from the sandbox right through today. Then, say an additional for-

giveness affirmation for anyone you may have forgotten. You can also forgive institutions, political parties, governments, etc. However, remember that people run these organizations. When all the layers are peeled back, it is still a relationship that we are talking about: It is still a person or persons you are forgiving.

HOW DO I KNOW I NEED TO FORGIVE?

You know you need to forgive someone if you feel (or think you might feel) anger, hurt and/or resentment toward them. The first person that popped into your head when you read this is obviously the person you need to begin with, and then proceed in the order that people come to your mind. I can guarantee you that the person with whom you're most angry, resentful and unforgiving will pop into your head immediately.

WHAT IF SOMEONE NEEDS TO FORGIVE ME?

If you have hurt someone and would like their forgiveness, you can use the forgiveness affirmation that I have provided at the end of this chapter. This affirmation is the same as the affirmation you need to say to forgive others, you're just replacing the words "I" or "Me" with the word "You," or their name. You can still free energy by saying this affirmation..

You can also forgive or be forgiven by those who have already passed on. Katharine decided to say an affirmation for her godfather, whose forgiveness she was seeking. She'd had an argument with him years ago and although her godfather had already died, Katharine wanted to seek release for an old emotional wound. She said she felt a sense of peace after saying the forgiveness affirmation and felt the past was healed.

Forgiveness Is Something You Do for Yourself

First and foremost, many people have many wrong ideas about forgiveness. They think to forgive means condoning the wrong done against them. They believe they have to contact the people who hurt them and get them involved. They think that forgiveness is something you do for the other people, that it's a selfless act. While all this sounds noble, it's simply not true.

First, forgiveness doesn't negate bad behavior. Forgiveness doesn't mean you agree with or accept how you were treated. Forgiveness is not to be confused with pardon. People should still be held responsible for their behavior whether it is immoral, unethical, illegal or all three. When you forgive, you are releasing yourself from this person and their actions on an energetic level. Forgiveness actually places power back in your hands. Forgiveness also doesn't mean you will allow that person to treat you in a manner you don't deserve again. Later in the book I will discuss the effects of forgiveness on justice. One of the most amazing discoveries I found in working with the forgiveness technique is that it actually allows for whatever justice is supposed to happen to move into place.

Second, you certainly do not have to get in touch with the person you're forgiving. Sometimes the people we need to forgive aren't around. They could be in other states, other countries or even no longer living. Those you forgive don't necessarily have to know you've forgiven them. The important thing is that *you* let go and free yourself from the anger and resentment. Most of my students and readers are so relieved when they discover they do not need to contact the people they plan to forgive. You can actually see the relief on their faces. When you make your list of the people you plan to forgive, you can use the forgiveness technique right in the privacy of your own home.

Finally, forgiveness is actually a "selfish" act. This doesn't mean it's a negative act. Far from being negative, it's one of the most loving and positive things you can do for yourself as well as for others. When people hear the words "positive selfishness," they think it's an oxymoron. We've been taught by our elders that being selfish is negative and harmful. It takes people a while to wrap their brains around the idea that the act of forgiving is to better their own life, that it is selfish in a way that brings good and happiness.

When you release old hurts and resentments, immediately new, fresh positive energy is made available to you to help meet your goals and dreams. When you feel more peaceful, your vibrational level changes in such a manner that those around you feel and benefit from it. They, too, may become more relaxed and easier to be around. The most amazing thing I have learned is that when you forgive it breaks the negative energy bond between you and the person of your unforgiveness. They are affected positively as well.

It is surprising to see the number of people in my workshops who are resistant to the whole idea of forgiveness. Many people have been nursing old hurts for so many years, they seem like companions. But I explain that forgiveness frees energy so that your dreams can come true. Forgiveness is not about other people, it's all about you and getting all that you desire.

Trisha was a participant in that class. Her first marriage had failed, and she blamed herself for it. In addition, she'd recently ended a relationship with a man when she'd caught him cheating. She had thought she would be marrying this man, and to top it off, he also owed her money. Needless to say, Trisha had some forgiving to do. Once she finally realized forgiveness would help her meet her own goals for the future, she was on board. Her goals were: a new relationship with a monogamous partner, a new job and a new house. Amazingly, she met a man with the attributes she was looking for in that very class. Considering that this was a small class, with only five participants, that feat was even more astonishing. Trisha manifested a new job right away and has now moved into her newly built home.

Forgiveness Breaks a Bond of Negativity

Although "unforgiveness" isn't an actual word, maybe it should be. We've probably all experienced "unforgiveness" at one time or another, by holding back forgiveness, and maybe even nurturing our hurt, anger or resentment. Unforgiveness acts as a kind of energy dam. The negative energy between you and the personal targets of your unforgiveness actually creates a steellike bond that keeps you tied to them. This negative energy attachment is stagnant and immobile, and keeps you from being your best self—it keeps you from achieving your highest good. Yes, lack of forgiveness keeps you literally "glued" in an energetic sense to the last person in the world you want to be harnessed to. It may be difficult to believe that sincerely repeating a simple affirmation can free you from your bondage, but it really *can* free you! It's been proven over and over by many of my readers and participants.

For years, Jenny had been having trouble establishing a meaningful romantic relationship. She also felt she was working in a dead-end job. Her troubles had begun after she had been terribly hurt by an ex-boyfriend, who she had not seen or heard from in eleven years. Jenny said the forgiveness affirmation, and the very next day her ex-boyfriend saw Jenny driving near her house. He followed her home, got out of his car, and said, "I've wanted to apologize to you for years for the terrible way I treated you in our relationship. I saw you driving by and for some reason just felt a strong urge to stop and tell you this. I don't expect anything in return. I just wanted you to know."

Jenny was absolutely shocked by this quick manifestation, but now feels she is on the mend and is actively looking for a new love for her life.

Upon Forgiveness, Energy Is Immediately Released to Bring You Goodness

When you invoke the Law of Forgiveness, the energy that has bonded you to another in a negative, stagnant way is immediately released. That energy is now free to flow into your life in a positive manner, bringing what you desire, and bringing the highest goodness to you. There are always positive results from this important action—from forgiving. Sometimes the results seem no less than miraculous.

After working on forgiveness using the specific method taught in this book, some participants received money and/or other valuables from people or sources they hadn't heard from in years. Businesses saw more customers, greater profits and general prosperity. Relationships improved, sometimes dramatically, and some severely broken relationships were healed. Participants said that individuals they had forgiven privately would call, e-mail or send them a check right out of the blue. The stories kept coming as more and more people discovered the positive benefits of using this important technique.

Kelly attended my workshop in January of 2002, and repeated the workshop after I added the forgiveness technique. She was the first participant who contacted me about the quick and astonishing results that can happen by using this tool. Since the January workshop, she had worked on several business goals with success. After using the forgiveness affirmation, she was blown away when she received a check in the mail for $25,000 from a ten-year-old lawsuit that had finally been settled.

After noting Kelly's success, Jim decided to try the technique to collect an old business debt. Jim was angry at a client who still owed him five hundred dollars after two years. At first, he was skeptical, wondering how saying a special type of affirmation could resolve this debt. However, since all else had failed, he decided it was worth a try. You can imagine his joyful amazement when he received a check in the mail from this client with the full payment one week later.

Breaking Negative Bonds Affects Others as Well

While the person(s) being forgiven may not know what in the world hit them, they will experience the effects of the negative bond being broken and energy being released. The effects on them are usually positive as well. Their hearts may soften in ways people who describe them can't believe. They may feel the sudden need to call, e-mail or apologize to you seemingly out of nowhere. People who interact with those they have forgiven through this affirmation say they are more positive, more pleasant and even nicer—some of them for the first time in years.

Jane had always experienced a troubled relationship with her mother, Mavis. She had never once heard her mother make a positive statement about anything. Jane struggled with self-esteem issues as she experienced constant berating. In addition to using the forgiveness technique, she decided to write a Law of Attraction goal affirmation to improve their relationship. She knew the Law of Attraction goal-setting method worked, because she had attended the workshop several times and was experiencing tremendous success in starting her own business. She had more free assistance and new customers than she knew what to do with. Her income was rapidly growing with no end in sight.

Regardless of her business success, Jane was nervous about trying the technique for her relationship with Mavis due to years of accumulated, deep hurt. However, she bravely pushed forward, did the affirmation, and scheduled a visit with her mother for the next week. After the visit, Jane told me it had felt almost surreal; Mavis exhibited a positive, upbeat attitude for the first time Jane could remember. Jane even asked Mavis if she had been placed on any medications to lift her mood. Mavis said that she had not been placed on medication and really didn't know why she was being positive, she just felt that way. Their relationship continued to improve. Jane later told me that when it was her mother's time to die, Mavis experienced a peaceful, loving and warm transition with her family by her side.

⬛ Contacting the Person You Are Forgiving

It is not necessary to contact the other person or persons for the forgiveness to work. For some people, it may not even be appropriate to make contact. You can freely forgive as many people as you choose without leaving your home. Many participants and readers are relieved when they learn they do not need to contact the other person.

Some people choose to contact the person, and that is fine, too. But again, it is not necessary to do so in order for the process to work. Usually, the person for whom the affirmation is being said is quite surprised to hear they are being so freely forgiven.

When April attended her first Law of Attraction workshop in 2004, nothing was going right. Her life felt broken, and as much as she tried, she felt helpless to pull it together. April had been molested by her father when she was a child and she still carried scars from that time in her life. To add to her woes, her marriage had failed, followed by a string of bad relationships, leaving her with a deep mistrust of men. She also had money and career problems.

April carried deep-seated anger against her father, who she had not seen or spoken to in three years. After enacting the forgiveness technique, the very next week, her father called and asked to see her. When he visited with April, he said something that most pedophiles never confess. He said, "I was wrong in my actions, and I know they hurt you. I am very sorry, and please forgive me." April was absolutely stunned and speechless. She said this interaction with her father has totally turned her life around. For the first time in her memory, she feels healed, whole and able to lead a happier life. Since that time, she has begun her own successful beauty and spa business. April has experienced such a tremendous transformation. She is now planning a career working with troubled young people teaching them the forgiveness method for healing. In addition, after saying the Law of Attraction relationship affirmation, she met her life partner, married him and now has manifested a dream house. She and her new husband are planning for a family.

You Do Not Have to Reconcile the Relationship in Order to Forgive

Forgiveness does not mean approval. It involves a willingness to see with new eyes—to understand and let go. They did what they did out of their own weakness. You did not deserve it. They could not teach you what they did not know. They could not give you what they did not have.   —Dr. Louise Hart, The Winning Family

This point is being restated because it is important. Forgiveness is something you do for yourself. It doesn't mean the other person was correct by acting in a way that hurt you. If they were correct, they wouldn't have wounded you in the first place. You may or may not choose to reconcile the relationship. **Forgiveness will work whether or not you choose to mend the relationship.**

It is also important to remember that forgiving someone is not presenting them with an open invitation to abuse you again. You are not condoning their behavior through this process of forgiveness. Forgiveness doesn't mean forgetting. You don't need to forget what happened to you—you only need to release its hold on your life. I'll be explaining the mechanics involved in using the forgiveness technique in Chapter 6. At that time, you'll set goals and list the attributes found in a healthy relationship. One of the relationship goals many people use is, "I now attract healthy relationships into my life." In listing the attributes of a healthy relationship, you may say that the person you're forgiving meets the following criteria: treats me with respect, values my opinion, is considerate and kind, and so on. As noted, we'll cover the technique in more detail in Chapter 6.

Repeat the Affirmation as Many Times as You Need

Most people want to know if saying the affirmation once is enough. Well, if you never see the person, it may be. However, if you are in frequent contact, they are likely to make you mad or hurt your feelings again at some point. So feel free to invoke the Law of Forgiveness as many times as you need, even every day.

Even if you're angry, resentful or are still experiencing the grieving process, I encourage you to continue saying the forgiveness affirmation. Remember, you are still activating energy and moving closer to achieving results.

Rhoda can definitely be described as a go-getter, and self-starter. She is a powerful woman who has begun several successful businesses over the years. When she talked about her husband, her anger was palpable. Her face flushed red, her teeth clenched, and her jaw tightened. She said that her husband had made some bad money decisions and wasn't holding up his end of the marriage in assisting her with their new home and businesses. She felt her businesses were suffering as a result with decreased profits. After Rhoda stated the affirmation of forgiveness and released her anger toward her husband, her business sales increased by 30 percent in one month.

Things seemed better until her husband lost a significant amount of money in a bad business deal. Rhoda's anger flared again. She was surprised that her increased resentment toward her husband corresponded with a drop in her business. Rhoda was going to write this off as coincidence but decided to try the Law of Forgiveness again. No sooner did she forgive her husband again than her business took a turn for the better.

Many people compartmentalize their lives thinking their business and personal relationships are separate. It is quite surprising how rapidly an increase in the success of a business happens after participants use the forgiveness technique for relationships.

Forgiveness Is Freeing

When you have sincerely invoked the Law of Forgiveness, you are releasing so much powerful energy, you can imagine a heavy burden is being removed from your shoulders. Now you feel lighter and freer than you have in a while. Enjoy the lightness, the vibrancy and the freedom this process brings.

Katharine had a dark childhood. She grew up in Manhattan as part of a family that had had great wealth for generations, stemming back to England. Her ancient family crest reads PEACE THROUGH WAR. This wasn't exactly a crowd actively seeking a tranquil lifestyle. Mostly raised by a nanny, Katharine had alcoholic parents who constantly fought, ignored their children and sued other wealthy relatives as a pastime and hobby.

By the time I met Katharine, her parents and most other family members had already died. Katharine had been so negatively affected by her childhood that it took her an entire year to fully work through forgiveness for her parents and family. Her businesses had become completely stagnant and she was in deep debt. She stood and walked with her shoulders slumped over, looking at her feet.

However, once Katharine was able to forgive, an immediate change took place. Her businesses improved and she felt as if a ton of pressure had been lifted off her shoulders. Her posture straightened, and she no longer looked at her feet when she walked. Her businesses improved dramatically and are literally booming. She has achieved more prosperity than she ever imagined. In addition, and perhaps more important, her life's purpose has become clear. (For more of Katharine's forgiveness story see the foreword.)

Many participants and readers have been surprised by how easy and effortless the forgiveness technique is—and how well it works. Those who had been angrily struggling with forgiveness issues for years became convinced that they had to "work hard and persistently" at forgiving in order to obtain any results. Most were frustrated and disillusioned because after years of trying everything they still were "stuck" and had not received what they felt was their rightful due, or hadn't met their goals.

Jamie was one of those disillusioned people who had tried for years without success to receive child support payments. Jamie had set her original Law of Attraction goal, and it was to receive $1,000. She had been in the class for two weeks when she said the affirmation of forgiveness. The very next week, she received a check for $500 from her ex-husband. The extraordinary thing was that her ex was an unemployed musician and had never sent a child support payment in thirteen years. The second half of her Law of Attraction goal was met when she realized $500 in savings when she purchased a rare item she had desired for some time. It is truly remarkable that the forgiveness technique Jamie used was able to accomplish what all the lawyers could not.

Once you've witnessed the tremendous transformation forgiveness can bring to your own life, you can teach others. Stacey had been working with the technique and experienced such astonishing results, that she decided to pass the technique on to her neighbor. She sent me this note in an e-mail:

Hi Connie:

I wrote my neighbor's forgiveness affirmation for her. I told her it works for you and is about you, not the person who hurt you. She had gotten a bad settlement from her ex-husband and had been struggling with money for years. She wrote him a letter and told him it was unfair and how she has been struggling, etc. After she used your forgiveness technique, her ex-husband called her out of the blue and bought a house for her. The reason your technique is so mind blowing and amazing is that their divorce was eleven years ago. It was not until she said her forgiveness affirmation that he stepped up to the plate. The house goes to the grandchildren when she dies. I'm telling you, that's big energy moving there. Your forgiveness technique works!!!!! Thanks for sharing these major life-changing tools!!!!

Gratefully yours,
Stacey

Self-Forgiveness

The remarkable thing is that we really love our neighbor as ourselves; we do unto others as we do unto ourselves. We hate others when we hate ourselves. We are tolerant of others when we forgive ourselves. It is not love of self but hatred of self which is at the root of the troubles that afflict our world.
—Eric Hoffer

It is at least as crucial to forgive yourself as it is to forgive others. When you forgive yourself, energy is free to come into your life, bring your highest good and manifest your desired goals. Both Trisha and April said that working on self-forgiveness for their failed relationships was an important part of their healing process.

Many people feel angry or guilty for mistakes they may have made years ago. They let yesterday prevent them from enjoying today, and they allow it to determine their tomorrow. They may even find it easier to forgive others as opposed to forgiving themselves. These accumulated resentments may cause problems in every area of life: money, relationships, job/career and health. Lack of forgiveness for self may cause people to harbor low self-esteem and a feeling of unworthiness. These negative feelings can determine how they vibrate, which in turn determines who and what they attract into their lives. If they are vibrating low due to harboring unforgiveness for self, they may keep attracting the wrong relationships, the wrong jobs or careers, etc. If you find yourself attracting the same old negative jobs, friends, significant others, bosses, etc., even though you've moved three times and changed jobs four times, then it's time for some introspection and self-forgiveness.

The Law of Forgiveness is a tool that you can use anytime you need to "let go" and free yourself through forgiveness.

How to Enact the Law of Forgiveness

When I refer to the Forgiveness Affirmation Technique, I am talking about the process described below. You will say this affirmation for anyone you wish to forgive, anyone you wish to forgive you, and to forgive yourself. The forgiveness affirmation that follows will be used for everyone from the sandbox up to today to release energy that will become available to assist you to meet you goals and dreams. You do not need to reconcile or continue the relationship in order to use the forgiveness affirmation. In Chapter 4, I will introduce you to a three-step technique to positively affect difficult relationships. This three-step technique will incorporate the Forgiveness Affirmation Technique in addition to two other steps. It will be used for relationships you wish to reconcile, improve or continue.

Make a List

It is helpful for some people to make a list of those they would like to forgive. It doesn't matter if it takes you several days or weeks to work through your list. The important thing is you have begun the process. Make a list of everyone you can think of that you would like to forgive, from your present and your past. Also, make a list of people you have wronged, whose forgiveness you seek. Forgiveness works freely both ways.

Find a Quiet Space

First, set aside a quiet time when you are least likely to be interrupted. Turn off any disruptive electronic equipment. Make sure any people who live with you know not to interrupt and ensure your pets are settled. Sit or lie in a comfortable place and position.

Visualize the Person in Your Mind's Eye

Bring the person you wish to forgive into your mind's eye. As much as possible, see them happy and surrounded by healing light. Visualize their higher self, not their nasty, mean Earth self. If you have a number of people to forgive, you may wish to complete ... several sessions.

State the Forgiveness Affirmation

Bring each person into your mind's eye one at a time, and say the forgiveness affirmation to each of them. Next, visualize them smiling sincerely and accepting your forgiveness. When you say, "and all again is well between us," this means "the energy is now released." It doesn't mean you're now buddies. Next, see that person walking off a stage or out a door, and bring the next person into your mind's eye. You can say the affirmation aloud or silently. If you are forgiving a group, organization or country, picture the group in your mind's eye and state the forgiveness affirmation. You may even visualize the group members saying the affirmation to one another. To make forgiveness real, you must be sincere. It is recommended that you should state the affirmation as it is written, as it has proven so successful with numerous Law of Attraction and Law of Forgiveness students. Remember if you change the words around to continue to justify your anger such as, "I forgive you for not being the person I wanted you to be," or something similar, this means you are not willing to entirely "release" and "let go." Therefore, you will not receive the full benefits of complete forgiveness.

Affirmation to Forgive Others

I forgive you completely and freely, I release you and let you go. So far as I'm concerned, the incident that happened between us is finished forever. I wish the best for you. I wish for you your highest good. I hold you in the light. I am free and you are free, and all again is well between us. Peace be with you.

Affirmation for Others to Forgive You

[Name] forgives me completely and freely. He releases me and lets me go. So far as [name] is concerned the incident that happened between us is finished forever. [Name] wishes the best for me. [Name] wishes for me my highest good. [Name] holds me in the light. [Name] is free and I am free, and all again is well between us. Peace be with us.

Affirmation to Forgive Yourself

I forgive myself completely and freely. I release myself and I let me go. So far as I am concerned the incident that happened is finished forever. I wish the best for me. I wish for myself the highest good. I hold myself in the light. I am free and all again is well with me. Peace be with me.

Take a deep breath! You did it!

Daily Forgiveness

When you have worked through your forgiveness list, you can use this technique any time you need it. You may even want to practice forgiveness daily just to make sure everything is straight. Catherine Ponder in *The Dynamic Laws of Prosperity* suggests that you practice forgiveness every day. She says:

Sit for half an hour every day and mentally forgive everyone that you are out of harmony with, feel badly toward or are concerned about. If you accused any of injustice, if you have discussed

anyone unkindly, if you have criticized or gossiped about anyone, if you are legally involved with anyone, mentally ask their
forgiveness. Subconsciously, they will respond. In like manner, if
you have accused yourself of failure or mistakes, forgive yourself.
Forgiveness can form a vacuum that will undam your prosperity
and success.

If you don't have thirty consecutive minutes to spend, then spend
five minutes either when you awaken and/or before going to sleep.
Once you have memorized the forgiveness affirmation, you may
repeat it whenever you have time—when you're bathing, driving,
eating or engaging in other routine activities.

Expect a Miracle

People have reported results from saying the forgiveness affirmation
in as little as five minutes, although it can take a few hours, or a few
days or a week or more. For some people it takes longer and that's
fine. Some results seem to be miraculous. I believe miracles are standard occurrences that science hasn't caught up to. When they can
finally be explained by science, they won't even seem unusual. They
happen because the laws of the universe do not need our scientific
understanding to operate. We do not need to understand a law in
order to set it in motion and experience results.

The miraculous results people are experiencing with the forgiveness technique are worthy of in-depth examination. Many of my colleagues agree that the flow of all energy in the universe, including
the energy freed up when we enact forgiveness, will one day receive
a scientific explanation. In other words, miracles are actually normal
occurrences, based on the natural laws of the universe.

Scientific Evidence for the Power of Forgiveness

Once the effectiveness of forgiveness became apparent, I began to research the literature; I wanted to understand these occurrences that appeared to be miracles. During my search, I found scientific research studies about forgiveness. However, I wasn't able to find any research about people being able to manifest dreams and goals including material rewards, as a result of forgiving. The area of focus in the published studies was how forgiveness could improve a person's overall mental, emotional and physical well-being. None of the studies researched how the forgiveness process worked. However, I did find that forgiveness is definitely a topic of interest for the scientific community, and there are serious studies being conducted in this area.

Studies on Forgiveness

Dr. Fred Luskin, director and cofounder of the Stanford University Forgiveness Project, conducted research on forgiveness with college-age adults, younger- to middle-aged adults, cardiology patients, and Catholics and Protestants from Northern Ireland who had lost family members to political violence. He describes in his book *Forgive for Good: A Proven Prescription for Health and Happiness* how his first study found that people who were taught to forgive became less angry and felt less hurt, and in fact developed into people who were more optimistic, compassionate and self-confident. These "forgivers" weren't carrying around as much anger on a daily basis, and didn't accumulate anger, either. Dr. Luskin's other studies found a reduction in the experience of stress, physical manifestations of stress and an increase in vitality.

Luskin also writes about studies conducted at the University of Tennessee and University of Wisconsin, Madison, which found physical health benefits related to forgiveness, including fewer medically diagnosed chronic conditions, lower blood pressure, less stress, and fewer physical symptoms from illness. Subjects participating in forgiveness studies report less depression, an improved spiritual connection and an overall improvement in physical and mental well-being.

Dr. Luskin is one of many researchers who worked on A Campaign for Forgiveness research, which was an organization that supported scientific studies about forgiveness. The John Templeton Foundation and others have donated seven million dollars, funding forty-six innovative research projects on the effects of forgiveness. The campaign's executive director, Everett L. Worthington, Jr., Ph.D., stated:

> Until recently, the tools of science have not been employed to investigate forgiveness. The new wave of research we've begun, however, has the potential to reveal the profound value of forgiveness in our lives—information that could reduce human misery and increase the quality of life worldwide.

Dr. Worthington, a psychologist, began studying forgiveness in the 1980s while working with troubled couples. Then he experienced a personal tragedy which increased his passion about the study of forgiveness. On New Year's Eve 1995, his mother was murdered. Afterward, he put his grief into action by writing books, publishing studies, and launching A Campaign for Forgiveness. Through this organization, he has raised millions of dollars, distributed to researchers nationwide for the study of forgiveness.

Most research in this area has focused on the psychosocial and emotional aspects of forgiveness. However, some scientists are studying the mind-body connection of forgiveness, or how forgiveness can affect the whole person. Dr. Tom Farrow, a clinical psychologist from the University of Sheffield, in the United Kingdom, studied the effects of forgiveness on the brain. Farrow is fortunate to live in England where brain science is one of the top areas targeted for medical research. In 2001, Farrow and colleagues used a type of brain scan called magnetic resonance imaging (MRI) to look for changes in blood flow when research subjects were presented with scenarios involving forgiveness and unforgiveness. They discovered that when a person forgives, increased activity can be seen in a portion of the frontal lobe of the brain—this area is responsible for emotion, problem-solving and complex thought. Forgiveness also affects a posterior area of the brain, which is associated with imagery and memory.

Dr. Pietro Pietrini, chair of clinical biochemistry at the University of Pisa Medical School in Italy, studies how human behavior and emotion are determined by the brain. The preliminary results of his research show that the areas of the brain responsible for moral judgment, moral pain, emotions and decision making are involved with forgiveness. This is the frontal part of the brain, which is also responsible for the higher functions of thinking and reasoning. Some scientists believe that humans are hard-wired to engage in forgiveness in order to cooperate with others, allowing them to adapt to their environment, thus increasing their chances for survival. Frans de Waal, director of the Living Links Center at Emory University's Yerkes Regional Primate Research Center, believes that as mammals, humans are designed psychologically to learn forgiveness. He says, "It would be madness to jeopardize self-interest for the sake of aggression or fear toward another, and so all mammals develop a certain strategy for survival: the capability to get over their hostile feelings."

Thus far, my own research is based on case studies and is anecdotal in nature. Therefore, the results cannot be generalized as if it were a carefully conducted, peer-reviewed scientific study. However, I have collected enough case studies with similar results that they bear mentioning.

In the case studies of people who used the forgiveness technique I teach, the participants noted the expected improvement in overall mental, emotional and physical well-being; they also noted an improvement in manifesting material goals and dreams. None of the research studies I reviewed reported an increase in participants manifesting tangible goals and dreams. However, they may not have found an increase in manifestation of material goods because they were not looking or testing for this variable, as those studies focused on physical, emotional and mental well-being.

As a side note, the participants who choose to interact with the people they have forgiven report finding the recipients of forgiveness easier to get along with, and altogether more pleasant than before. None of the studies currently on the books reported the effect on the person(s) being forgiven. Again, this was not a variable that was considered in the studies I read.

Because forgiveness belongs to the psychological, social and emotional realm, I also considered that forgiveness might only improve a person's life in these areas. I knew that forgiveness would help people to feel better and improve their relationships. I knew that a lack of forgiveness could negatively affect their relationships. But I had no idea that a lack of forgiveness could block goals in every area of a person's life, including money, job and career development. It also blew my mind that a person's forgiveness could positively affect the person they were forgiving even when they did not contact them. This makes me realize that much more needs to be done in the area of forgiveness research. It is my hope that the forgiveness technique I have developed can be studied scientifically.

How the Forgiveness Technique Works

I have always been a person who was not satisfied with a description that defines *what*—I'm a person who wants to know *how*. Don't just tell me what it is, tell me how it works! None of the studies in my literature review of forgiveness described *how* the process worked. For that information, I had to turn to quantum physics to understand the unusual results my clients were experiencing with the forgiveness technique.

I must admit that I was totally astonished when my workshop participants, coaching clients and readers started describing how people they hadn't contacted, but had forgiven in the privacy of their own homes, contacted them out of the blue—usually within a week. Some people even received phone calls and e-mails within minutes after saying the forgiveness affirmation; others were contacted within a few hours. One coaching client received four e-mails out of nowhere from people she had forgiven. They had not heard from many of these people in years. In addition, several people received checks in the mail from those being forgiven. On at least two occasions, the people being forgiven even showed up in person after an absence of years. Many reported receiving checks in the mail from other sources after they had used the forgiveness technique.

I knew that forgiveness is a law of the universe and therefore these seemingly strange occurrences could be explained by science. I just wondered if science as we understand it had caught up with this amazing law. When I began to investigate, I was pleased to discover quantum physics is hot on the trail of explaining what happens energetically when someone forgives. I was able to add two and two together after asking workshop participants how many of them had experienced someone they knew calling them after they thought of that person—even people they hadn't heard from in a while. When more than half the people in the audience raised their hands, I knew the same law was operating behind the forgiveness technique. Somehow not only was energy released but information was exchanged on a telepathic level—or what some people would call "a knowing level"—between the person forgiving and the person they forgave.

The phrase "quantum physics" can sound complicated and brings some of us memories of days spent in high school or college science classes just trying to understand anything the teacher was saying. I would many times wonder if the science instructor was actually speaking English, and if so, I would, at times, become concerned that I had suddenly lost my ability to understand English. So bear with me as I try to explain the concept of forgiveness, based on quantum physics, using basic language and my acquired knowledge of the topic.

In *Healing Words*, the author Larry Dossey, M.D., describes scientific studies that have been conducted on the healing effects of prayer, thought and meditation. In one double-blind study of heart patients on a cardiac unit in a hospital, it was found those who were prayed for experienced more healing, compared with those patients not remembered in prayer, and the differences were statistically significant.

Dr. Dossey also describes studies in which scientists were comparing the power of thought to the properties of radiation, to determine whether thoughts could travel through lead and would deteriorate at a distance. The scientists theorized that perhaps thoughts traveled in waves like radiation and held similar properties. In the studies, subjects sent their thoughts to petri dishes containing bacteria, fungi and even cancer cells. The subjects were separated from the petri dishes, which were in another room. The results were pretty astonishing—the subjects were found to be able to grow or shrink the organisms or cells using directed thought! The results were statistically significant when compared with a control group of organisms and cells that were not directed by thought. The scientists discovered that, unlike radiation, the directed thoughts could travel through lead and did not deteriorate at a distance. Even when placed in a lead room and then across the country from the petri dishes, the subjects were still able to affect the organisms and cells with their thoughts in the same manner.

Some scientists who study quantum physics believe these types of results can be explained through a holographic model of the universe. The holographic model also explains how, when a person is forgiven, she may suddenly be moved to contact the person forgiving her. With a hologram, all the parts contain the whole. This means the universe and everything in it forms a matrix or network so that anything that happens can be communicated everywhere all at once. In his book *The Divine Matrix*, Gregg Braden says, "The universally connected hologram of consciousness promises that the instant we create our good wishes and prayers, they are already received at their destination."

No telephone lines, Internet, e-mail or post offices are required. You talk about same-day delivery; we're talking about same-moment delivery! Our thoughts and prayers don't travel anywhere—they are already present at their destination.

To better understand the holographic nature of the universe, we can begin with our own bodies. Our bodies embody many holographic principles. For example, every cell, with the exception of the reproductive cells, contains the blueprint for the entire body. When each part contains the whole, it is holographic in nature. Our brains also function holographically. When a person sustains a brain injury through some sort of trauma such as a stroke, other parts of the brain will take over for the damaged or dead part. In addition, scientists have proven that when parts of the brain that were known for storing certain memories are destroyed or removed, the patient can still recall these memories. This means another part of the brain must also contain them—thus demonstrating its holographic nature. In *The Divine Matrix*, Braden continues by asking:

> Is it possible to live in a universe where the information between photons, the prayer for our loved ones, or the desire for peace in a place halfway around the world never needs to be transported anywhere to be received? The answer is yes! This appears to be precisely the kind of universe we live in.

Braden quotes Russell Targ, cofounder of the cognitive sciences program at Stanford Research Institute in Menlo Park, California, who says:

> We live in a nonlocal world where things physically separated from one another can, nonetheless, be in instantaneous communication. It's not that I close my eyes and send a message to a person a thousand miles away, but rather in some sense there is no separation between my consciousness and his consciousness.

Another principle of a hologram is that any change in one part affects the whole. This means your small act of forgiveness for even one person, not only affects that person, but actually affects the whole system or is felt in the whole universe. It also means if enough people forgive, the whole world will positively change in ways we can only begin to imagine.

This may sound a little strange to read in black-and-white, but in thinking about it, we've all had experiences that prove this principle in action. In addition to forgivers who have been contacted by those they forgave, or people who received a phone call from someone who came to their mind, but whom they hadn't heard from in a long time, there are many other examples of this principle being enacted. For example, we often hear about the experiences of identical twins, such as a twin who wakes up in the middle of the night experiencing chest pain while the other twin is thousands of miles away and is having a heart attack. There are many examples of mothers who wake up in the middle of the night just "knowing" that something has happened to their child. Many people report "knowing" the exact time a loved one passed away by experiencing some sort of mental, emotional or spiritual occurrence. I'm sure you can think of many other circumstances that can best be explained by the holographic model.

This principle is somewhat controversial because quantum research is a relatively new field of scientific study and the holographic model is a more recent theory. However, because scientific discovery is coming at such a rapid pace due to advances in technology, it is my hope that the older generation of established career scientists and some younger skeptics won't disregard the holographic model, but will instead support its full investigation.

Remember, the discovery of matches and lighters could not have happened without discovering that rubbing two sticks together in the right way can start a fire. The new generation of fertile young minds who were weaned on technology developed by the scientists and technicians before them could not perceive of "crazy sounding" ideas like a holographic universe if the previous generation did not lay the foundation. Sir Isaac Newton, who discovered the Law of Gravity when he was only twenty-four years old once said, "If I have seen further than others, it is by standing on the shoulders of giants." I encourage the scientific community and funding agencies to support fertile minds in their research of the holographic model of the universe. There is no room for ego that blocks positive progress when there is so much to gain.

Using the Law of Forgiveness to Heal Our Relationships

Using Forgiveness to Positively Affect a Difficult Relationship—A Three-Step Technique

All forgiveness, when the crusty layers are removed, comes down to a relationship, either with yourself or with others. As you've probably realized by now, relationships can be complex at times. We add layers of complexity with our expectations and our incompatibilities. Pretty soon we have built a huge wall layered with anger and resentment. Not a fun place to be. This is why I dedicate so much time in this book to forgiveness related to relationships.

Many people in my workshops, as well as those I coach, are having a difficult time with one or more people. I teach a three-step technique for positively affecting these relationships. People have reported a significant change in the relationship after using this technique. It is frequently used by people who are experiencing a difficult time with an ex-spouse, but it can also be used by those experiencing trouble with their bosses and coworkers, their children or other family members or friends.

The Three-Step Forgiveness Technique that I describe in this chapter has been used by many of my clients with quick and amazing results to repair relationships with family, friends, bosses, coworkers and others. In the Three-Step Forgiveness Technique, you will include the Forgiveness Affirmation Technique described in Chapter 2. For the FIRST STEP, you will write a goal affirmation for the relationship you wish to repair. For the SECOND STEP, you will use the Forgiveness Affirmation Technique described in Chapter 2 for the person you wish to forgive. For the THIRD STEP, you will have a soul-to-soul conversation with this person's higher self. This process is described in the following pages. I will also include an example of an action plan using the Three-Step Technique by one of my coaching clients so that you may gain an idea of how it works.

To clarify again, the forgiveness affirmation described in Chapter 2, you will use for everyone to release energy so that your goals and desires will manifest. The Three-Step Forgiveness Technique you will use only for those relationships you wish to improve and/or reconcile. Both these techniques can be completed in the privacy of your own home without contacting the person you are forgiving.

Step One: Develop a Goal Affirmation for the Relationship and for Any Blocks and Barriers

First, you must say an affirmation stating the attributes you desire in the relationship and when you would like to see those attributes. This is your goal affirmation. One attribute may be that they show you basic respect. This was true for Terry, who was having a difficult time with his ex-wife. Terry also desired to spend more time with his young son, Mark, and he wanted his ex-wife, Heather, to stop speaking negatively about him in front of his son. Additionally, he was seeking to have his child support reduced. He developed these specific affirmations for his goal:

My relationship with Heather now has the attributes of respect, kindness and fair treatment by _____.
goal date

Heather now speaks positively about me in front of our son by

_____.
goal date

I now have eighteen overnight visits with my son per month by

_____.
goal date

My child support is now _____ per month by _____.
                      amount   _goal date_

Goal affirmations should contain only positive, forward-moving words. They should be written as if they have already manifested, and with a goal date for manifesting. They should *not* contain the words *will, want,* or *intend*—or any negative words such as *debt-free, pain-free* or *addiction-free.*

In addition to a goal affirmation for the relationship, you develop affirmations for any psychological blocks or barriers. These are affirmations addressing any underlying thoughts or feelings you may have regarding why the goal hasn't already manifested. Psychological blocks or barriers are any excuses you can think of regarding why your goal hasn't already manifested. For example, if your block is: "My ex-husband is a deadbeat who never keeps a job and doesn't pay his share of the child support," your affirmation for the block would read: "My ex-husband is now employed in a well-paying job that he enjoys and he pays his child support in full and on time." Another example may be an ex-husband who thinks his wife is using all his child support payments on herself to go to the gym and spa. Thinking these negative things about his ex-wife would be an energy or psychological block or barrier. He would turn this block around into an affirmation describing what he really desires. He would say: "My ex-wife is using all the child support money I send to meet the needs and well-being of our children. She understands the importance of and honors our legal agreement. She uses her income or other sources only to meet her needs and desires."

When Terry began stating these affirmations along with implementing the second and third steps of this technique, he was amazed only one week later at the fast results. When he arrived to pick up his son, Heather didn't have one negative comment about him in front of Mark. She agreed to the eighteen overnights per month and Terry's child support payments were reduced by half.

Step Two: State the Forgiveness Affirmation

The second step is to sincerely state the forgiveness affirmation found in Chapter 2 for the person you're concerned about. Even if you're still angry, this is an important step and will move energy in a positive direction.

Step Three: Have a Soul-to-Soul Conversation

Lastly, in the privacy of your own home, have a soul-to-soul conversation with the person whom you're forgiving. This is similar to the forgiveness affirmation. You don't need to contact the person. Find a quiet time when you can be alone, comfortable and undisturbed and bring this person into your mind's eye. Just like with the forgiveness affirmation, visualize their happy, higher self, not their mean, nasty Earth self. Visualize them in a happy and smiling state, as you imagine they would look if they had treated you as you desired. Then, you will have a soul-to-soul conversation. You can pour out your heart to their higher self. You can say exactly what you felt went wrong and how you wish things to be resolved. You can say exactly what you wish to say, and you can feel free to be totally honest. You can pour out your heart and soul; you can visualize their higher self accepting what you have to say with kindness and compassion.

The PESC Technique

Some people would like to know how best to approach the soul-to-soul conversation discussed above. I have found the PESC technique to be extremely useful for people who feel a need to communicate with others about a problem. Not only can it be used in soul-to-soul conversations, but it works very well with people who must be confronted in person. The PESC is an acronym for:

P—*Problem*

E—*Emotion*

S—*Solution*

C—*Consequences*

At the "P" stage, simply state the *problem* that concerns you. With the soul-to-soul conversation, you can really go into detail because you are talking to the person's higher self. Remember that a person's higher self does not judge. This means their higher self will be supportive and will not reject you or what you have to say. If you can imagine the person looking peaceful, kind, caring and angelic, then you can imagine their higher self. You may also choose to write a letter to their higher self. For some people a letter assists them in clarifying their thoughts.

In the "E" stage, describe how the problem makes you feel—find the *emotion* that the problem evokes. There are four basic ways you may feel: mad (angry), sad, bad or glad. Every emotion you can think of generally fits into one of these four categories. This is an integral part of your soul-to-soul conversation, but it is also quite effective in communicating with others. The reason this technique works well is that people cannot deny *your* feelings. This technique is commonly known as using an "I" statement. You say, "When you _____(X), it makes me feel _____(Y). The "X" part of the statement allows you to describe the problem; the "Y" part lets you state how the problem makes you feel. The good thing about using an "I" statement is that it helps prevent the person you're communicating with from becoming defensive, in contrast to what happens when using "you" statements. "You" statements automatically place people on the defensive—and when we become upset, most of us automatically head straight for a statement that begins with "you." For example, "You never listen. You are selfish. You hurt me terribly. You can't be trusted. You always lie to me." The person at whom a "you" statement is directed has little choice but to defend themselves. Their defense is generally followed by their own set of "you" statements—and these are directed back at the person who started the "you" accusations. Once each person becomes defensive, most productive communication stops.

As part of the Three-Step Forgiveness Technique for handling difficult relationships, you can use "I" statements made to the higher self of the person you're forgiving. They will not judge you, so you don't need to become anxious, or feel as though you're walking on eggshells, trying to word each sentence in just the right way.

Traditionally, "I" statements end after the speaker states the problem, and identifies how it makes them feel. However, if you explain a problem without offering a solution, it may slow progress toward your goal. Therefore, the "S" in the PESC technique stands for *solution*.

When communicating with the person's higher self, you will explain your idea for a solution. Feel free to go into detail and pour your heart out. Remember, a person's higher self does not get bored, so you may talk as long as you like. Also, feel free to write a letter to the person's higher self if it assists you in clarifying your thoughts. (Should you approach someone in person, it's important to state your solution as clearly as possible. If you have time, develop a solution in advance to help smooth the communication.)

After describing what you perceive the solution to be, you must communicate what will happen if no solution is reached. This is the "C" in the PESC model and stands for *consequences*. In this stage, you will explain to the higher self of the person you are forgiving what the consequences will be if the solutions you have offered are not considered and if the problem continues unabated. (If you should approach someone in person, you will need to be honest in what the consequences will be if they are not willing to solve the problem.) Next, you imagine in your mind's eye the person's higher self accepting your communication and solution. You may also wish to imagine them replying with positive and supportive statements about your viewpoints.

A short example of a conversation using the PESC approach is given here:

When you spend more money than we make, month after month, the increasing debt makes me feel unsure, angry and frightened about the future. I would like to suggest that we sit down together and develop a monthly budget and a plan for paying off our debt. If you continue to overspend without a budget,

I will continue to be very concerned and may need to consider other options for the future.

This is a very shortened example of how to use the PESC technique to discuss a topic that is relevant for many couples. No doubt your conversation with the higher self of your partner/spouse will be longer. However, this should give you an idea of how to word the conversation to include PESC.

Reaching Relationship Goals

In *Law of Attraction: Develop Irresistible Attraction*, I provide details about how to write a customized action plan, which lets you achieve results quickly. In this action plan, you choose one to three goals to work on at a time. (I do not advise working on more than three goals at once, or you may become overwhelmed.)

Working through this action plan will help you reach your relationship goals quickly. Below, you'll see an explanation of the method used, and the actual Law of Attraction action plan that Terry (who we met earlier in the chapter) and I developed specifically for him, to help him reach his relationship goals. You may wish to develop your own action plan, following these six steps. There is a blank form on pages 75–77 to record your action plan.

In **Step 1**, list the topic area of your goal. There are generally four areas in which people have goals: money, relationships, job/career and health. In this example, Terry would like to improve a relationship he is in, so that is the topic area for his goal.

In **Step 2**, develop your goal affirmation using only forward-moving, positive words. Include a date that you believe is reasonable for reaching your goal.

Step 3 has two parts: in the first part, you'll list all psychological barriers to reaching your goal, and the feelings the barriers evoke in you; in the second part, you'll take all of these reasons, or excuses, and turn them around.

For Step 3, Part A, use a separate piece of paper to list any psychological blocks or barriers that are keeping you from reaching your goal. Examine your heart and mind closely. Look for any underlying thoughts and feelings that you have about the goal. Spend some time assessing these. Ask yourself why your goal hasn't already been achieved, or why your dream hasn't come true. You may record any number of excuses, or what you may have been thinking of as reasons. An excuse is any sentence that begins with these, or similar, words:

But . . .

If only . . .

I can't . . .

It will take too much . . . (effort, time, money, skill . . .)

I'm too busy, too tired, too young, too old, too fat, too thin, too short, too tall, etc. . . .

It never happened when I tried it before . . .

Some common excuses I hear in my workshops that are specific to relationships:

All men/women are jerks, flaky, cheaters, just want your money, etc.

I've had bad past relationships—you don't understand—very bad past relationships.

You can't trust ex-spouses/partners; they're just out to get you and what you have.

Exes try to turn your children against you.

Exes spend all of their time hatching plans to ruin your life.

My ex is spending all of my child support money buying stuff for herself and her new significant other; my children aren't getting a dime.

And the list goes on.

Each time you list an excuse, also write the associated feeling beside it. In other words, if you write: "My goal hasn't come true because I think my ex-spouse is an unreasonable person," also write, "This makes me feel angry and frustrated." Using this tool, you should be able to assess your thoughts and your feelings, and clearly state any issues that you believe are preventing you from manifesting your goal.

For **Step 3, Part B**, you're going to take all of the excuses you just recorded, and turn them around. This is important because negative excuses can act as psychological and energy blocks or barriers. They can literally block your goals and dreams from manifesting. In this step, write down *what you desire*, instead of writing down *what you do not desire*. For example, if your ex won't pay child support payments, your affirmation for that particular energy block might read: "My former husband gladly pays his child support payments on time, and in full. He is healthy, able and prosperous, making more than enough income to easily cover child support. He understands completely that these payments are for the positive welfare of our children. He is able and willing to make child support payments on time and in full."

Write down these affirmations turning around all of your blocks and barriers under a heading called **Affirmations for psychological/ energetic blocks/barriers.**

In **Step 4** of the action plan, create a to-do list. In this list, write down the action steps you plan to take to make your goal come true. In your to-do list, include the number of times each day that you will repeat affirmations for energy blocks and barriers. I strongly encourage you to repeat the affirmations a minimum of three times a day. Also, make a list of those you wish to forgive, and record a commitment to state the forgiveness affirmation for each of those people. Remember to write down a commitment to say the forgiveness affirmation for yourself and for those from whom you wish forgiveness; don't forget to include your soul-to-soul conversation. Write down additional action steps that you need to take in order to make your goal come true. The action steps are very important; it's not enough to sit on the sofa or lie on your bed and think, "I'm positive, bring it on." You must show up, be present, and work your to-do list in order to manifest! I remember when one client said, "This is more than just repeating an affirmation; it's going to take some work, isn't it?" The answer to that question is a resounding YES! This journey will require both external and internal work on your part, but it's so worth it!

In **Step 5** of the action plan, list synchronicities (smaller manifestations) that prove your desire is manifesting. If your goal manifests quickly, like Terry's does in the upcoming example, you may not experience any synchronicities, or smaller, incremental manifestations. If your goal takes longer to manifest, you will notice occurrences that seem like coincidences that are related to your goal. For people who have studied how the Law of Attraction and Law

of Forgiveness work, we know there really are no coinciden...
What may appear to be coincidences are really experiences we have attracted into our lives for one purpose or another. When you state your affirmations, complete your forgiveness work and complete your to-do list, energy begins to move. When it does, small manifestations will often occur, telling us that our goal is on its way to completion.

As an example, a woman who attended one of my Law of Attraction workshops several years back had developed a goal to grow her business. During the third week of the four-week workshop, she said that the local newspaper had contacted her; they wanted to feature her in an article as the top black businesswoman of the entire area. She asked if this was a synchronicity. I said, "Well, I should say so." This area is home to over a million people, and a feature article that would reach that kind of readership would definitely help her to manifest her stated goal.

In Step 6 of the action plan, write down the date and time that your desire manifested into your life, and record how you felt about it. This is a very important step: When you list the date and time, and your feelings about your desire, it gives you a historical perspective going forward. You will want to record your progress and what it took to get there. This will assist you as you meet additional goals in the future. Since I don't recommend that you work on more than three goals at a time, as soon as you meet one goal, you can add another if you so choose.

If you're like me, you can best understand instructions if you can see an example. This particular action plan is Terry's plan for dealing with the difficult relationship he was having with his ex-wife, as well as a plan for meeting some goals he had for his relationship with his son. Reading through the example will assist you as you develop your own action plan. In Terry's plan, you'll see that his forgiveness affirmation and his soul-to-soul conversation are included as part of Step 4 (the to-do list). This is the same format that all of my Law of Attraction students/clients use to meet goals in all areas of their lives. I would highly encourage you to use this same format and create your own action plan if you need to make positive adjustments to a relationship.

Terry's Law of Forgiveness Action Plan

Goal Number 1

Step 1: Topic area for the goal: Relationships.

I (Terry) would like to improve my relationship with my son's mother (Heather) and Heather's husband (Max).

Step 2: Goal affirmation, using positive words (must be specific, measurable and must include a goal date).

My relationship with my son's mother, Heather, now has the following attributes (see listed attributes), which are supportive of us raising our son.

ATTRIBUTES:
Heather is respectful and supportive of my time with our son.

Heather is flexible, both with schedule changes and with increasing my time with our son by August 31.

Heather is respectful toward me on the phone, in person and in front of our son.

Heather is reasonable; there has been a change in child support payments so that the amount paid is the amount that was originally agreed upon.

Heather is more loving and respectful toward our son.

[Note to reader: If, like Terry, you are raising children with an ex-spouse, you are still in a relationship with them, even though it is a different kind of relationship than it was when you met. Therefore, I would highly suggest that you develop a goal affirmation for the attributes you would like to see in that person, or in that relationship.]

Step 3: Affirmations for psychological/energetic blocks and/ or barriers:

[Terry identified the energy blocks and barriers, the feelings that go with the blocks and then turned the blocks around]:

I am now supported by my son's mother, Heather, and her husband, Max, and have a more flexible relationship and visitations with my son.

Heather now understands that treating me with dignity and respect is important and healthy for our son's well-being.

Step 4: Action plan (to-do list):

State my affirmations three or more times a day.

State the forgiveness affirmation for Heather.

State the forgiveness affirmation for Max.

Have a soul-to-soul conversation with Heather's higher self explaining what I would like to experience in my relationship with my son, how she and Max can support me and why it is important for our son's well-being.

Have a soul-to-soul conversation with Max's higher self explaining what I would like to experience in my relationship with my son, how he and Heather can support me and why it is important for my son's well-being.

Step 5: Synchronicities (smaller manifestations) that prove your desire is manifesting:

[Terry manifested so quickly (in only one week), that he didn't really see any smaller manifestations before the big one.]

Step 6: Date/time your desire manifested into your life and how you felt:

Within a week after beginning to say my affirmations, I could hardly believe the positive change in Heather's attitude. This almost-immediate manifestation of my desire was remarkable. Heather acted much more respectfully toward me, was nicer and didn't display a bad or hurtful attitude when I went to pick up our son, Mark, for my weekend visit. She agreed that I could see our son more often. Also, my child support payments have been reduced.

▓ Goal Number 2

Step 1: Topic area for the goal: Relationships.

I (Terry) would like to have a better relationship with my son.

Step 2: Goal affirmation, using positive words (must be specific, measurable and must include a goal date).

I now have flexible, easy visits with my son that equal eighteen overnights or more per month by August 31.

Step 3: Affirmations for psychological/energetic blocks and/or barriers:

I am now supported by Heather and Max to have a more flexible relationship and visitations with my son.

I now have time for this relationship.

Step 4: Action plan (to-do list):

State my affirmations three or more times a day.

State the forgiveness affirmation for Heather.

State the forgiveness affirmation for Max.

Make time in my schedule for additional visits with my son.

Have a soul-to-soul conversation with Heather's higher self explaining what I would like to experience in my relationship with my son, how she and Max can support me, and why it is important for our son's well-being.

Have a soul-to-soul conversation with Max's higher self explaining what I would like to experience in my relationship with my son, how he and Heather can support me, and why it is important for my son's well-being.

Step 5: Synchronicities (smaller manifestations) that prove your desire is manifesting:

[Terry manifested so quickly (in only one week), that he didn't really see any smaller manifestations before the big one.]

Step 6: Date/time your desire manifested into your life and how you felt:

I reached this goal one week after putting my plan into action. I am extremely happy with the results and changes that took place. I could hardly believe Heather's reaction to me, when we interacted during our first visitation after I said the affirmations. She was pleasant, treated me respectfully, and was willing to work with me so that I could see my son more. We worked out a schedule that permitted me to see Mark the exact number of days I had written in my goal. I felt happy and relieved that I would be seeing my son more often.

Here is a blank form that you can use to develop your own action plan. Feel free to follow this format as you write or type your plan.

Repeat your affirmations at least three times each day. Some people find it more convenient to write or type their affirmations on note cards and carry them around so they remember to say them. Work on your action plan's to-do list daily, and remember to look for and record any synchronicities that prove that your goal is on its way.

Law of Forgiveness/Law of Attraction Action Plan

(Complete a separate form for each of your desired goals. Remember, this works best when working on one to three goals at a time.)

Step 1: Topic area for the desired goal (money, relationships, job/career, health):

_____

_____

_____

_____

Step 2: Affirmation for the desired goal (use positive words, be specific, make sure the goal is measurable and include a goal date):

_____

_____

_____

_____

Step 3: Affirmations for any psychological/energetic blocks and/or barriers:

_____

_____

_____

_____

Step 4: To-do list for making your desire manifest (include "I state my affirmations _____times each day [minimum of three]):

_____

_____

_____

_____

Step 5: Synchronicities (smaller manifestations), which prove that your desire is manifesting:

_____

_____

_____

_____

Step 6: Date/time that your desire manifested into your li
and how you felt when it happened:

_____

_____

_____

_____

Expect Amazing Results

After reading about Terry's experience, and his results, it may seem like it all happened very easily. The truth is that Terry was as surprised by his quick results as anyone would be. He had such a difficult relationship with his ex-wife that he thought they might never agree on anything again. But Terry was so motivated to see his son that he really focused on his goals and completed the work in his action plan. As a result, he reaped the benefits in a very short period of time.

Like Terry, many of my workshop participants and coaching clients report the most amazing results after completing the Three-Step Forgiveness Technique for handling difficult relationships, previously discussed, especially when this technique is included as part of their Law of Forgiveness/Attraction action plan. People have reported great results when they used this approach with significant others. It seems to be especially helpful when working with relationships with ex-spouses. But this technique works well with parents, family members and friends as well. What follows are examples of different relationships that can be healed by the Law of Forgiveness/Law of Attraction action plan and success stories for each.

Forgiving an Ex-Spouse

Donna is an amazing woman who is fully committed to the Law of Attraction journey, and she's bringing all of her friends along for the ride. While going through a divorce, Donna successfully used the Three-Step Forgiveness Technique (Chapter 4) to positively adjust the attitude of her ex-husband in only two weeks and after only four hours of workshop instruction. Here's Donna's story:

> My ex-husband and I went to mediation in February. He was very negative and did not comply with meeting his financial commitments to me. After I used the strategies you teach, including specific affirmations and the three-step forgiveness technique, he called me, on June 21st. I could immediately hear that there was no attitude in his voice. He was calling to ask where to mail the check, so he could get it in the mail that day! Needless to say, I am thrilled! I think some of his attitude was because he thought that I would have hatred and resentment toward him, due to all the circumstances, and he was ready for it. Surprise! No hate or resentment here, and I truly think he didn't know how to react! The techniques you teach WORK and are truly amazing!
>
> As far as my desired relationship (which I affirm that I have), I am saving the very BEST for last. I have let go of the past, and my heart and head are free and radiate love and happiness wherever I go, and to everyone I meet. It "feels" wonderful!

I just received an update from Donna and indeed she has manifested her desired relationship. This is what she had to say:

Hi, Connie,

Well, I won't be attending your "How to Attract Your Perfect Partner Through the Law of Attraction and Law of Forgiveness" workshop on May 7th. All I did was sign up for your workshop, and he found me! I put my affirmation away "somewhere" and when I find it, I will go into more details about all of this for you. About a month ago, I just decided to also add, "God I know my life is in your hands." I have always said, "God works in strange ways," and this is truly one of those ways. I will share more with you soon. Thank you for your help in guiding my "thoughts" in a positive direction. I "fell off the wagon" for a while, but when I started again it worked better than I ever imagined! I am living the "happily ever after" that I always dreamed of, with no doubts.
God Bless You!

Live, Love, Laugh,
Donna

Forgiving Significant Others

Susan attended my Law of Attraction workshop and right away manifested a financial goal, receiving unexpected checks that totaled more than $1000 and a weight-loss goal of six pounds in one week. However, she said the most meaningful goal was when her husband of eighteen years told her for the *first time* that he appreciated her. Susan said her husband was a man who found it hard to express his feelings, and this statement blew her away. Even to this day when she tells this story, her heartfelt emotion is overflowing.

Relationship goal—My goal here was to feel nurtured and appreciated in my marriage. After eighteen years of marriage (and for the first time ever) my husband told me "out of the blue" that he really appreciated me and all that I do and that he probably doesn't say it often enough.

I have been a student of the Law of Attraction for quite some time. I have never had such amazing results or such a clear path on how to achieve them so quickly. I know I will continue to use these processes over and over with better and better results!

Forgiving Your Parents

Nate's Forgiveness Story

While most of my clients are middle-aged, I also find it easy to work with young adults. They tend to be open-minded and more willing to use the forgiveness technique, as compared to some of my older clients who have decades of accumulated anger and resentment. Nate is a young man I met in a grocery store. I noticed that he was no ordinary clerk. He had a beautiful smile, a friendly nature, was very smart, and seemed to take a genuine interest in each of his customers. He enjoyed talking with his customers and he soon confided in me that he was in his early twenties with big forgiveness issues. He was very angry with both of his parents. They had totally cut off his money supply at the very beginning of the semester in his junior year of college. They weren't happy that Nate had made a D in one of his classes even though he had also earned an A in one, and Bs in the rest. As he spiraled into near-bankruptcy, Nate had to drop out of college and get a low-paying job in a grocery store. He also lost the place where he was living and his car. Nate was angry that his parents compared him with his older sister who had made high grades in college despite a learning disability. He didn't understand his parents' extreme reaction and ended all contact with them for a year and a half.

I told Nate about the Law of Forgiveness and encouraged him to try the technique. Feeling depressed and agitated inside, Nate was very open to the idea of forgiveness, realizing the anger and resentment he was harboring was negatively affecting all areas of his life, including his job and relationship.

One month after saying the forgiveness affirmation, he was completely surprised by an unexpected visit from his father. Nate had never told his dad where he was employed, which made the visit even more of a shock. His father had come to ask Nate to watch for a check in the mail, as one should be arriving soon. Nate noticed the interaction with his father was much less awkward and more relaxed than previous encounters had been. His father even shook his hand and gave him a hug.

In addition to financial rewards, Nate also received a job promotion with a much better schedule. His supervisor asked him to manage the store in his absence, and he is being groomed for another promotion to a managerial position. After two years of struggling, Nate is most surprised by how much his life changed in just two short months after saying the forgiveness affirmation.

I'm happier, more relaxed, have more energy and my relationship with my girlfriend has improved. I can let little things go that used to irritate me. The forgiveness technique places you in control of things instead of becoming a martyr. When life presents future challenges it's good to know I have a tool that is so simple yet so powerful.

Three months after reconciling with his father, Nate's good fortune continued when his mom called on his birthday. They made a lunch date, and reunited after not seeing each other for two years. As a secondary benefit, this reconciliation led to a manifestation of an additional $34,000 from an account his mother had opened for him. More recently, he unexpectedly received $30,000 from a business venture.

This influx of income allowed Nate to consider other options for his life and work. He will be taking a new job in information technology, more in line with his talents and passion. He will also be taking a long-needed and well-deserved vacation with his girlfriend, and is even considering a move to another city. Nate also reunited with his extended family for the first time in several years while attending a party for his grandparents.

Kelly Ann's Forgiveness Story

Kelly Ann was young, smart, beautiful and ambitious. She was tall and slim, with blonde hair and blue eyes. Even though many would have thought she was the stereotypical beauty who never had a problem getting a man, Kelly Ann had not been able to manifest a relationship in over two years. In my workshop, when Kelly Ann talked about her parents, she was so angry that her face turned red and the anger she felt inside seethed through and was apparent in her voice. Kelly Ann was really furious with her parents. She felt her parents didn't understand her, didn't care about her, and didn't have time for her.

Kelly Ann was open to the concept of forgiving. She had a desire to reconcile her relationship with her parents. She visited them and shared the forgiveness technique with them. She said that for the first time, she felt her parents really heard what she was saying and understood how she felt. Kelly Ann also began to understand her parents' perspective; how they oftentimes had not meant to ignore her, but had felt overwhelmed by their own lives and responsibilities. When I saw Kelly Ann for a private consultation after her reconciliation with her parents, she looked like a different person. I had to look twice to recognize her. She was literally beaming. Her face had softened and was no longer red when she spoke.

Kelly Ann said she had manifested a job right away after forgiving her parents, but was still working on manifesting a relationship. Then, she called to cancel our next appointment a week later because she had indeed manifested a new relationship with a wonderful guy she'd met at her new job. She was off to the beach with him. Kelly Ann even signed her mother up for my Business Abundance workshop and her mother began meeting some of her own dreams and goals.

Forgiving Other Family Members

Kim had never attended one of my Law of Attraction workshops, or read my book, *Law of Attraction: Develop Irresistible Attraction*, but she found an article I had written about forgiveness on a website. Kim was able to use the forgiveness technique with amazing results after just reading the article.

After reflecting on the article, I decided to follow its advice and try to forgive some family members who have hurt me and my two sons deeply. Spiritually, I knew I needed to forgive them, more for my sake than theirs, but I was both skeptical and intrigued by the idea that offering forgiveness would free up energy to manifest blessings in my life as well. I'd been living "on the edge of a breakthrough" for years, and was really ready for it.

Within three weeks of saying the affirmations for each of the people I needed to forgive, I was able to resolve a work situation that has resulted in a raise and a lot more opportunities; I received a check for $53,000 from a client who hadn't paid in months; I got more business for my home-based consulting business; and best of all, I started a relationship with a wonderful man I met months ago, but who didn't ask me out until after I'd done the forgiveness exercise. Maybe all these things would have happened anyway, but I choose to believe there's a connection here!

Forgiving Friends

I was teaching the Three-Step Forgiveness Technique for addressing difficult relationships at an introductory Law of Attraction workshop when I noticed a beautiful young woman in the front row with her hand raised. Kara introduced herself and said that she'd read my article on forgiveness on my website the night before the workshop. She decided as she was lying on her bed the evening before to say the forgiveness affirmation for a friend she'd had a fight with. The fight had been very disturbing for Kara; she was going through a divorce and this friend had been a big comfort to her. The loss of this friendship was a big blow. Kara said that within minutes of completing the forgiveness affirmation for her friend, the phone rang and, sure enough, it was her friend. Not only did they mend their relationship, but they planned to attend a concert the next weekend with music they knew would be healing for both of them.

Friendships are such an important part of our lives. I know as I was growing up boyfriends came and went, but my best girlfriends stuck with me through thick and thin and we're still there for each other until this day. Friendships really are very important and we need to nourish and cherish each of them. Some of my clients have a goal to make new friends. I assist them in writing their affirmation with the attributes they would like in the friends they meet. I have found this an easy goal for my clients to meet. They always come back several weeks later for their coaching session with several new wonderful friends they have already met and socialized with.

I encourage everyone to write an affirmation for friends with a list of attributes you would like them to have. When you are actively practicing forgiveness and working on your goals, you raise your vibratory rate. Three things will happen. First, some of your friends will raise their rate to meet yours (or maybe their rate is already high). Second, some friends who aren't quite ready or do not wish to raise their rate will leave your life because they don't feel quite comfortable around the increased vibrations. Third, new friends vibrating at the same rate will enter your life.

Friends truly are golden so if you're ever experiencing a problem with a friend, the Three-Step Forgiveness Technique is an excellent tool for you to use to bring that relationship back into balance.

But I'm Still Angry . . . Working Through the Cycle of Healing When Forgiving

The Cycle of Healing

One question I frequently get from workshop participants and readers is: "What happens if I still feel angry or hurt after saying the forgiveness affirmation? Should I say it anyway?" The answer is. . . **absolutely!** Saying the affirmation places forgiveness in your mind, heart and energy field. You still reap the benefits of the energy and with forgiveness energy around you, you will begin the healing process.

If you're angry and hurt, even while you're using the forgiveness technique, it's likely because you are still grieving that loss and you need to go through a healing process. Remember, the fact that you need to forgive someone means a transgression was committed against you. You've been hurt, wronged, maybe even traumatized: there are a lot of negative emotions surrounding the person and situation that require your forgiveness. And although the forgiveness affirmation is very powerful, it won't necessarily take away all the pain that may have been building up for years.

It takes time to heal. Not only have you been had, but every transgression causes us to experience a sense of loss. It could be a material loss, the loss of a relationship, but it's always a sense of loss on an emotional level. When someone you know betrays you, there is a loss of trust. If you are the victim of a crime or physically injured, there is a loss of a sense of safety. Even when you have to forgive yourself for a mistake you may have made, there is a loss of self-respect.

Much has been written about the stages of healing. The most accepted model is the one developed by Elisabeth Kübler-Ross, who studied grieving associated with the death of a loved one. However, Kübler-Ross and other mental health practitioners discovered that no matter what the loss, it is predictable that most people go through five basic stages of grief: shock and denial, anger, bargaining, depression and, eventually, acceptance.

Depending on the person's coping mechanisms and support system, they may move through these stages fast or slow. People do not always proceed through the stages in perfect order and at a steady pace. Sometimes they make a step forward and two steps backward. Some people do not experience every stage. It is important to be patient with yourself when you are experiencing the grieving and healing process. It is also important to seek the resources you need to assist you during this time: mental health and other practitioners, support groups, supportive family and friends, your faith tradition and whatever positive coping mechanisms that work for you.

In *Forgive Your Parents, Heal Yourself*, Dr. Barry Grosskopf suggests joining a support group that will bear witness to your pain. He says:

Support groups provide a safe place to risk the openness because members have experiences in common. They can understand each other's experiences, compare and contrast them, and make sense of their feelings in each other's company, thereby breaking free from the bonds of their former isolation. They become each other's healers as each member gives comfort to the others, and to the extent he/she is open, allows comfort from others. The very act of joining such a group is a return from isolation to the fold of [human]kind.

One of my favorite books on this subject of healing is the classic bestseller *How to Survive the Loss of a Love* by Melba Colgrove, Ph.D., Harold H. Bloomfield, M.D., and Peter McWilliams. Bloomfield, a psychiatrist, and Colgrove, a psychologist, take you step-by-step through the grieving and healing process on the left pages of the book. On the right pages of the book, Peter McWilliams supplies his wonderful poetry to ease you through each step of the healing process. By combining knowledge that is helpful with good poetry to express the feelings involved, the authors have given all readers a powerful gift. This classic was first published in 1976, and has been updated periodically. I have gifted it to more people experiencing a loss than I can remember. And I have to say that I can't count the number of times I've read it myself in my young-adult days, agonizing over the loss of one more romantic relationship that bit the dust. I find it just as timely and useful today as it was then.

Not only do Colgrove and Bloomfield provide wise advice for healing throughout the book, they view loss as part of the natural order of existence. This means that even loss is governed by the laws of the universe. They say:

In nature, loss is an essential element of creation—the rose blossoms, the bud is lost; the plant sprouts, the seed is lost; the day begins, the night is lost. In all cases, loss sets the stage for further creation (or more accurately, re-creation). So it is in human life. It's hard to look back on any gain in life that does not have a loss attached to it.

While understanding that loss is an inevitable and necessary part of life does put things into perspective, it doesn't erase the pain when loss inevitably happens. That is why we all need tools with which to heal from loss, and a support system or community of caring in place to help us. However, in regard to losses that occur in relationships, it does help to know that, in even our worst relationships, there was learning and growth—even when the only thing we learned is what we *don't* want in a partner, friend, supervisor, etc.

The forgiveness technique is an important tool we can use for healing. While using this technique will not replace the work needed to proceed through the healing process, for many people, it can make the process easier and faster. You may keep repeating the forgiveness affirmation the whole time you're healing. Over time, the overwhelming feelings associated with the loss will lessen. This doesn't mean you will ever forget what happened, but you know you have forgiven, released the pent-up energy, and you are able to move forward with your life. This process leads to acceptance, the final stage of the healing process. Many people report that when they have reached this stage and think about the person of their unforgiveness, they no longer experience negative feelings. Some people report feeling released and at peace, and other people report no longer experiencing any feelings associated with this person or event.

One of my workshop participants said that he had enemies who had disrupted his business and his personal life for years. He said at first he was hesitant to forgive these people who had made his life so miserable. However, he desired to improve his business and make more income, so he was willing to try anything positive to reach his goals. He said a feeling of total calm and peace came over him after he forgave. He reported that he was amazed when, almost immediately after using the forgiveness technique and repeating the forgiveness affirmation, his enemies just went away; they didn't contact him, and were no longer in his life. He asked me to explain how a process like this could work so fast and effectively. I explained that when he *sincerely* forgave his enemies using the power of his words through an affirmation, and felt the powerful feelings of calm and peace, a few things happened immediately. On an energetic level, we are electromagnetic beings. An electrical current of energy is responsible for our every heartbeat. Our brain lights up with electrical activity any time we think, process or experience feelings and emotions. We resonate with energy. Like a roomful of tuning forks all humming the same energetic notes, we attract people into our lives who vibrate at the same level we do. As stated previously, when we forgive our past, we release the negative energy holding us back, and our vibratory level increases. The people in our lives will either raise their vibratory level to match ours, or they will leave our life, as they will no longer be comfortable being around us. People with a higher vibratory level, one that matches ours, will enter our lives. This explains why my workshop participant's enemies left almost immediately after he forgave. They no longer matched his energy vibratory level. This doesn't mean our vibratory level will always remain high. To keep it high, we must work at it every day by forgiving, and exposing ourselves to positive experiences.

If you think this sounds like so much mumbo jumbo, I invite you to think back and reflect on things in your own life. It's very likely that you'll find many examples of this as you examine your past. For example, focus on remembering when something extremely positive happened to you, such as getting into a great college, getting a much sought-after job, earning a promotion, embarking on a new career, finding a new partner or spouse or welcoming a new baby. Do you remember how you felt? You may have been so happy you felt as if you were walking on air. How did those around you react to your success? Did any of your friends leave your life afterward? If so, what did you attribute this to at the time? Did you brush it off, attributing it to the fact that you were now too busy to continue the friendship, or you had a different focus, or maybe you even felt that your friends were jealous? It is true that your focus may have shifted with the new positive changes, but consider this: When you progressed, your vibratory level increased. You may have even felt more energetic and excited. Any of your friends who could not adjust to this new level no longer felt comfortable being around you, and simply left or drifted away. With time you may have noticed that new friends came into your life who shared your excitement and new interests.

Going forward, you may notice that, after increasing your vibrations, you no longer feel comfortable around certain old friends. Some people even use the terminology, "We just don't seem to match anymore." They have hit the nail on the head. The vibration levels of people in these situations just don't match anymore, which can make one person feel out of sync with another person. If you're in that situation, you may find that you no longer enjoy the other person's company the way you used to. Many people scratch their heads when this happens. They have trouble defining what has occurred. Many even grieve the loss of old friendships. I encourage people to appropriately grieve all losses as this is normal and will assist you to heal. However, understanding the reason behind the loss may make it easier to accept.

This phenomenon is also true when your vibration level is low or has decreased. Have you ever experienced a rough patch in your life where you had little self-esteem, felt needy, unworthy and/or depressed? Maybe, to make matters even worse, you found out that your significant other had cheated with your best friend. You noticed that everyone at work was picking on you, and was full of negativity, much of it directed toward you. Your relatives were needy and were constantly asking you for money and favors. You felt like the cartoon guy who's walking around with a rain cloud over his head, while everyone else experienced sunshine. Your life was worse than a country song! There's a joke that says if you run a country song *backward,* you get your spouse, your dog and your house back. Like the main character in a good country song, you were wondering what went wrong. The answer is simple. You were vibrating at a very low level and attracting low vibratory circumstances into your life. So, how would you turn it around? How do you run the country song that has become your life *backward*? To change your life, you must raise your vibrational level. Using the forgiveness technique is a good place to begin this process. You can also use the Three-Step Forgiveness Technique for handling difficult relationships , described in Chapter 4, and you will be absolutely amazed at how quickly the people in your life respond to the energetic change you create.

Anger and Forgiveness . . . Can They Coexist?

Another question that I'm frequently asked is: "What if I live with the person and I feel angry all of the time, because of their behavior?" Again, my suggestion is to use the techniques I have explained in the section entitled, "How to Use Forgiveness to Positively Affect a Difficult Relationship—A Three-Step Technique," in Chapter 4. After using this technique, I can't promise you which way the relationship will go. Sixty percent of clients reported that their relationship improved, and forty percent reported that their significant other became more distant. However, I can assure you that when you follow this technique for several weeks, your energy will change in such a way that the target of your forgiveness will move one way or the other. If they move away, that will at least give you information with which to make your next move when you're ready. Remember, you're always in the driver's seat—meaning that you don't have to make any moves until you're ready.

Martha was referred for a private session by another longtime Law of Attraction student. Martha was definitely one of those people whose life had turned into a country song. She said that she often listened to Patsy Cline, an old-time country singer who sang from her heart and soul about her love for a man she believed to be less than faithful. Martha questioned her husband's faithfulness to their marriage. She looked sad and depressed, and sat slumped in her chair. She had a difficult time making eye contact when she spoke. Martha said that she and her husband had had a long marriage with very traditional roles. Martha told me that she loved her husband very much, and wanted more than anything to feel understood, valued and cherished. Her desire was to feel happy and successful in her marriage. For years, she had felt like she'd been meeting everyone else's needs, while neglecting her own. Martha was very open to using the Three-Step Forgiveness Technique, described in Chapter 4. She was amazed to discover that she could energetically alter the behavior of a man who had not changed in almost a half-century. After several private sessions with Martha, and one with her husband, Bill, I received an e-mail from her saying that Bill was acting in new ways, ways she had not witnessed in their entire forty-two years of marriage. She said:

> Bill still amazes me. He walked on my just-mopped floor yesterday, and left a trail of dirt. He actually apologized. I bought him a new

shirt over the weekend. He wore it to work today and called me this morning to thank me for it. This may not sound like much to others, but it is to me. He has never been thoughtful of my feelings in the past forty-two years of marriage. He actually listened to my office drama without telling me he doesn't want to hear it if I'm not going to do anything about it. So he must have actually listened to you. I look forward to spending more time with the "new Bill."

Thank you more than you can know,
Martha

I continued to meet with Martha, once each month. After several sessions, her entire countenance changed. I was supposed to meet Martha in a coffee shop and walked right by her table, as I didn't recognize her. She was sitting upright in her chair with a broad smile on her face. She was almost glowing. I love to witness this kind of change in my clients. When they forgive and use the tools I provide them with, they look different. It reminds me of that scene in *Beauty and the Beast* when the evil spell is broken, and the dark castle, black, and brooding, is all of a sudden flooded by light; bright colors emerge, birds chirp, and it becomes beautiful and glowing.

Martha's appearance was now beautiful and glowing. She had developed an inner confidence that came shining through. She continued to smile throughout our conversation and had no trouble making eye contact. The transformation was amazing.

This *doesn't* mean that her husband had suddenly become the handsome prince and they lived happily ever after. There's an old Chinese saying, "After the ecstasy, the laundry." The main problem with Hollywood is that they show *"the ecstasy"* of the moment when the prince and princess kiss and decide to become one, but they never show *"the laundry"*—the lifetime of work that makes for a successful relationship. What it *does* mean is that Martha now had tools which she could use to better her life, and she had the knowledge and confidence with which to use them. She continued to make improvements, and at the same time continued to experience real-life situations. For example, several months later, Martha's father died. Martha had been her father's primary caregiver for many years while he was ill. She was angry and devastated by his death, as well as by the loss of her role as his caregiver. However, now she had tools that would let her cope with the grief, anger and loss she was experiencing. Utilizing these strategies prevented Martha from sinking into despair.

When going through the cycle of the healing process, it is important to understand what it means to be angry, and to recognize the importance of releasing that anger. Author Gary Zukav says, ". . . beneath anger lies pain, and beneath pain lies fear." He believes we use anger to resist feeling pain. Gary says that we use anger in resistance to the world, life and other people not being the way we want them to be. Gary continues by saying:

> Rage is an excruciating experience of powerlessness. Striking out in rage is an act of powerlessness. Obtaining revenge and proving guilt are expressions of despair and helplessness. Like the small animal that attacks the larger animal, you have given up hope. There is nothing left to do—except experience what you are feeling. Acting on anger, rage, vengefulness are your last resorts. They never work. The world continues to be other than you want it to be and the pain of that does not diminish. Instead, your anger increases.

Gary believes you should move beneath the surface of anger and find out why you are in pain. When you address that pain through forgiveness and healing, you begin to transform your life.

Dr. Robert Enright, a licensed psychologist and professor of educational psychology at the University of Wisconsin, Madison, states that he created the first scientifically proven forgiveness program in the country. In his book *Forgiveness Is a Choice: A Step-by-Step Process for Resolving Anger and Restoring Hope,* Dr. Enright lists four phases in his guidelines for forgiving. He believes that in the first phase, the forgiver must uncover the source of anger before moving to the second phase, which is deciding to forgive. He bases his approach on research studying anger and forgiveness. His third and fourth phases involve developing an understanding for the person you are forgiving and noticing how the process of forgiveness has changed you now and how it will change you in the future.

In his literature review, Enright found several researchers who have studied the relationship between forgiveness and anger. Issidoros Sarinopoulos is one researcher who asked four hundred people to complete questionnaires about forgiveness and anger. Not surprisingly, his study found that the more people forgave others who had deeply hurt them, the less angry they felt. He also found that those who forgave family members who had hurt them deeply had less heart disease (diagnosed by a physician) when compared to those who didn't. Kristy Ashleman and Gayle Reed studied divorced women and men. In her study as a graduate student, Ashleman studied thirty divorced women and found that those who had forgiven their ex-spouse had a higher sense of well-being, lower anxiety and lower levels of depression. Reed studied men and women whose ex-spouses had been unfaithful. She discovered similar results: Those who had forgiven and found meaning in their suffering had higher well-being and lower anxiety levels when compared with those who did not choose to forgive.

Through studying the research of others and conducting his own research about forgiveness, Enright concluded, "When someone is exceptionally angry, forgiving can offer an effective antidote."

Thank Goodness

When you're still reeling with feelings of anger at people who have wronged you, in addition to using the forgiveness technique, it helps to sit down and work on a gratitude list. Every day, list on paper, or to yourself, three to five things you are grateful for in your life. I kept a gratitude journal for a year, each day listing three things I was grateful for. It made a tremendous difference in my outlook. If you don't like to journal, then go through your gratitude list in your head. Now, I go through my gratitude list anytime I am angry or down and feeling sorry for myself. When engaged in the process of gratitude, you will find that you are, in fact, a very fortunate person.

You're the Writer, Producer, Director and Casting Agent of Your Own Real-Life Hollywood Production

You may not live in Hollywood, but if you can imagine your life as a feature film, stage play, soap opera, sitcom or maybe even a show straight from Comedy Central, you will greatly expedite your understanding of how you may have created melodrama in your life. The Law of Attraction teaches us that we have attracted everything we are experiencing in our life—both the good and the bad—through our thoughts, feelings, prayers, actions, inactions and soul-level decisions. It's not your bad childhood, God or the universe, or your ex-spouse or ex-lover that has placed you in the starring role of the current life situation. Like in the movie *The Wizard of Oz*, you are the man behind the curtain pulling the levers and pushing the buttons that are creating your grand reality from moment to moment.

You may ask, "If I'm creating my own reality, how did all these irritating people show up in my soap opera? This is my life! Why would I bring them here to drive me crazy?" That's simple—you cast these people in their parts. That's right—you're also your own casting agent.

People are attracted to you and react to you not based on how you *feel about them* so much as how you *feel about yourself*. When you start enacting the Law of Forgiveness and begin vibrating at a higher level, those people will either change to vibrate at your level or they will leave your life, and new people vibrating at a higher level will take their place.

Colin Tipping is an author, international speaker, workshop leader and radical forgiveness coach. In his book *Radical Forgiveness: Making Room for the Miracle,* he states, "Ninety percent of healing occurs when you become willing to let in the idea that your soul has lovingly created this situation for you."

Tipping believes that we create our experiences, both good and bad, for soul-development purposes and that we attract people into our lives that show us the parts of our being that need healing. He recommends that the forgiver should express gratitude to the person that they need to forgive for showing them the lesson their soul needs to learn.

He believes that if we learn the lessons, then we don't keep repeating them. However, if we don't learn, we keep creating the same scenarios over and over with a different cast of characters.

So, if you don't like your soap opera or the script you have written and the actors you have cast, the good news is that you can change it. You can change it by changing your thoughts, feelings, actions, self-talk and by working on forgiveness. The first step is developing the awareness, and then accepting the responsibility for the life you've created.

Rose-Marie was one of my very first Law of Attraction students. She had quite an epiphany upon discovering that she was the person responsible for so many of her dreams not being met. When she accepted this responsibility and started "working on her stuff," she manifested her dreams and goals. Several years after that first Law of Attraction workshop she wrote:

> Connie's approach to transformation grabbed 100% of my attention from the first class. I remembered and utilized many strategies from the class but one particular group conversation stands out from the rest. With Connie's facilitation, the group explored the concept of "boulders." Are there boulders in our lives blocking our energy that we are not even aware of, or more likely, and worse, that we intentionally placed in the way of our own highest good? My answer to that question was a definite, "yes." It was a moment of disequilibrium for me to take responsibility for not achieving so many of my personal dreams such as a truly loving relationship and a loving family. I was also very unhappy in my job at the time. I remember the discomfort of owning my part in not allowing myself to permit the very things I wanted the most to come into my life. Connie gently guided the group through a process in which everyone took away just what they needed to create change and transition.

After taking personal responsibility, and forgiving herself and those in her past, Rose-Marie's whole life changed. She manifested her life partner, found a career that was more satisfying where she works from home, and is now the mother of two lovely children. This kind of personal transformation begins with awareness, then willingness to take responsibility, and last but not least, a willingness to change.

The Law of Forgiveness
at Work

Using the Law of Forgiveness to Land
the Job of Your Dreams

The majority of the attendees at my Law of Attraction workshops attend for one of three reasons: more money, better relationships or a job. And I've found the Law of Forgiveness can help with all three.

I'll never forget a woman who attended one of my first workshops looking for a job. She said she had sent out 100 resumes over the last month and a half without one single return call. When I asked her what she thought was the reason she had not received a call for an interview, she said that she was a stay-at-home mom for seventeen years, she had no skills and wondered aloud who would hire her. Can you pick out the blocks and barriers in her self-talk? First, I assisted her in developing an affirmation listing the attributes of the job she desired and the people she desired to work with. Her goal date was at the end of the month, which coincided with the end of our workshop. The workshop met for four consecutive weeks, and each session was two hours. Second, I helped her write an affirmation to turn her blocks and negative self-talk around. Finally, I taught her to do her forgiveness work. Just two weeks later, after only four hours of instruction, she said she had received four phone calls asking her to interview, and by the fourth and last session of the workshop she had a job.

I had another client who liked his life's calling as a counselor for troubled youth but didn't like the poor pay or the demands of the administration where he worked. He developed an affirmation that he was self-employed as a counselor for youth and young adults setting his own hours and making a larger amount of money (and he wrote the amount of money he desired) with a goal date for manifesting. Within several weeks, he'd manifested everything he desired when he was hired as a civilian contract employee to work with our military servicemen and -women. He also provides other contract work on the side and more than doubled his salary compared to his previous employment. Needless to say, he is very excited about his career and his future.

While there are always a few people at my workshops looking for a job or a career more in line with their life's passion or purpose, it was just this year that one of my coaching clients called and asked if I would develop a workshop designed especially for people who were looking for work. With the economic downturn, hundreds of thousands of Americans are seeking employment. I developed a workshop entitled Using the Law of Attraction/Forgiveness for Job Finding and Career Enhancement. Job-hunting support groups have formed around the county where I live, and I have delivered the workshop to some of these groups with very positive responses. People who are out of work tell me they are feeling afraid, frustrated and worried. They thank me for giving them tools that have been proven to work with thousands of my workshop participants, coaching clients and readers. These tools place them back in the driver's seat and give them a greater sense of control over their situation.

I recently saw a participant who attended my last job-finding workshop when she attended another workshop I offered called Using the Law of Attraction/Forgiveness for Attracting Your Ideal Romantic Partner. She said the forgiveness technique has worked so well for her that she is blown away. She received phone calls, money and opportunities right away after beginning to work through her list of people to forgive. She sat in the Singles' Workshop with a look of positive shock and awe the whole time with her mouth open just like she couldn't believe all the good things that were happening in her life so quickly.

These are only a few of the countless stories of how people achieved career goals and experienced increased income after using the techniques I teach, including enacting the Law of Forgiveness. Through the act of forgiving others and themselves, they opened themselves to receive all sorts of opportunities.

You're Hired

When I met Roberta she was a single mother struggling to support herself and her young son. She harbored a lot of anger: against the company that had laid her off the year before; against the companies she interviewed with that didn't hire her; and against herself for her inability to land a job. But most of all, she was angry at her past, which she blames for her current situation.

Through the Law of Attraction workshop, she learned she needed to forgive and release her anger if she was ever going to move forward. She was significantly motivated to forgive those in her past when she discovered it would assist her to obtain the job she so needed.

She requested a private session with me so we could properly word her goals and go through the forgiveness techniques. We worked together for an hour and the very next day she e-mailed me with the great news:

> I got THE job. I did exactly what you told me to do but I did it this morning because I fell asleep last night before doing so. They are going to call me back today to tell me the exact pay, however, she did say it was more than my last job. The supervisors were in a meeting, therefore, they all needed to meet about the salary. She also stated that I will probably start during the week because they have to get me a computer, phone, etc.
>
> I want to thank you today for sharing the class, sharing your time, sharing your wisdom and being the person you are, because if you were negative in any way, you would have lost me. Remember when I told you I wouldn't talk when I was a young girl, well, see I love to talk NOW—therefore, I can share with others about you and send business your way with my testimony. Now, I can get back to taking spiritual classes and don't forget that for the future. You just don't know how I acted after my coaching session with you last night when I got home. I was very hyped, so hyped that I was dancing around, singing, etc. You have that kinda effect. You did that for me in the class, too, after I left each week. Keep doing what you do because you do it so well. Thank you again, Connie, for taking your time at that time of night for the coaching session to help me make one of my dreams come true!

Roberta said that utilizing the Law of Attraction and the Law of Forgiveness in her life every day had given her the tools to overcome any obstacle in her way. Roberta is well on her way to ensuring a better future for herself and her son.

Forgiveness Helps You Move Ahead and Move Up

Carey had been working for the same company for six years and he was beginning to feel stuck. Over the years he watched several of his colleagues get promoted while he remained in the same old job doing the same old thing. He felt tremendous resentment toward his boss who he felt was overlooking him unfairly and he was downright angry at one of his coworkers. Carey believed that Melinda, who was part of his team before she was promoted to management, took the group's ideas and presented them as her own. Their project was a group effort, but Melinda, who of her own initiative took a leadership role, seemed to get all the credit.

In our Law of Attraction workshop, Carey expressed frustration that no matter what he did, he seemed unable to manifest success at work. But upon talking through his situation, he came to realize that his negative feelings were blocking the success he deserved. Willing to try the Law of Forgiveness, Carey did everything I suggested: the Three-Step Forgiveness Technique for handling a difficult relationship, the Law of Forgiveness/Law of Attraction action plan; he even kept a gratitude journal.

No surprise to me, but certainly to Carey, he was promoted to a newly created position within weeks. The new job utilized his strengths and promised plenty of opportunities for both personal and professional growth and the best part was that his new job came with a hefty raise.

Using Forgiveness to Become More Productive at Work

As a freelance writer, Gail's income was dependent on magazines picking up her articles. But lately, she seemed to have trouble coming up with ideas, and even when she did have a viable idea, for some reason it took her forever to write it. Was it writer's block? Gail hoped not; she needed to keep the creative juices flowing in order to keep the money coming in.

When Gail attended one of my Law of Attraction workshops she had three goals: to buy a townhome, to get a new car and to find a relationship that was solid and dependable. She had divorced two years ago when her husband cheated on her. She blamed him for her current situation. He was always behind on her alimony payments and all she could afford on her own was a small studio apartment rental. She drove around in a ten-year-old car that was always breaking down and was not reliable.

One day after class, I chatted with Gail, asking her how things were progressing. She confessed that she was frustrated. She had been on several dates but she described them all as "losers," and with her writing barely generating enough money to pay her rent, she didn't see how she would ever be able to afford to buy a car, no less a townhome. As we spoke, she continuously brought up her ex-husband and how he "totally messed up" her life.

I reminded her of the Law of Forgiveness and suggested she work through the Law of Forgiveness/Law of Attraction action plan to let go of her anger against her ex-husband. Although she wasn't sure if she was ready to forgive him she agreed to give it a try. It was a long process for her, and when the class ended she told me she would continue working through her anger to get to forgiveness.

About two months after the workshop ended, I received an e-mail from Gail:

I finally was able to do it! I was able to forgive my ex and let go of all the anger and resentment I had bottled up for so long. It feels so liberating! It's like a giant weight has been lifted off of my chest.

The best part is since I've forgiven, my "writer's block" seems to have cleared up. I've been writing up a storm and sold three pieces in one week. And, believe it or not, an editor from a publishing house contacted me after reading one of my articles. She wants me to turn it into a book! It's beyond what I ever imagined!

Oh, and I met the sweetest man in my new writers' group. I don't know where it will lead, but he's such a nice guy and I really like him.

Thanks for teaching me about the Law of Forgiveness. It's really changed my life!

Working with Difficult People: Forgiving Bosses and Coworkers

People who work eight hours or more a day at a single location may actually spend more time with their boss and coworkers than with their own family. Therefore, it becomes paramount to enjoy a harmonious relationship with those at work. Work life can become miserable when infighting and disharmony occur between coworkers. This kind of toxic environment can have a negative impact on health, happiness and productivity. However, the forgiveness technique can provide amazing results for changing the work environment from negative to positive.

Amy was working under very difficult circumstances for a boss who didn't understand her and wouldn't listen to her point of view. They fought constantly and Amy had decided she had no choice but to leave her position and find another job. Amy was very disappointed because she had long sought this position and enjoyed her work. She just didn't enjoy the constant tension she was experiencing with her boss.

Amy was quite relieved when she attended one of my workshops and discovered that she might be able to shift the relationship with her boss by using the forgiveness technique. I suggested to Amy that she use the Three-Step Forgiveness Technique described in Chapter 4. In addition to saying the forgiveness affirmation for her boss, Amy also developed an affirmation stating the qualities she would like to see in their relationship. Amy also had a soul-to-soul conversation with her boss's higher self.

When Amy returned to the workshop one week later, she was astonished by how the relationship with her boss had totally turned around. For the first time, her boss asked to meet with her to work out their differences. Their conversation was very productive and they came to understand that many of their disagreements were based on miscommunications and misunderstanding. Amy feels a ton of weight has been lifted off her shoulders since forgiving her boss. She now looks forward to going to work to a job she greatly enjoys. She finally feels validated and understood.

One of my coaching clients named Leon used the forgiveness technique for two coworkers with whom he was experiencing problems. He was amazed the next week when one of them e-mailed him and the other one actually stopped by his office and asked to work out their differences. He didn't go to them, they came to him! Leon says that now when he becomes stressed out at work by coworkers, he uses the forgiveness technique to help him feel more relaxed and in control.

Using the Forgiveness Technique to Build Business

Many business builders have used the forgiveness technique with success to increase their sales. Coaches and counselors have used it to achieve fast results with their clients. Network marketers have used it with their downlines. Many times people are excited about the products they're selling and want to sell, but personal issues, such as lack of forgiveness, are tripping them up. The forgiveness technique helps to move energy and get sales flowing faster than any strategy I have ever seen.

The Forgiveness Technique for Entrepreneurs

Tom attended a Business Abundance for the Entrepreneur workshop I presented for people interested in beginning their own business. After participating in the workshop exercises, including the forgiveness technique, he was very surprised to get a call only one and a half hours after completing the workshop. Tom was especially amazed because he hadn't officially begun his business and his first customer was already calling.

Within one and a half hours after leaving the workshop this evening, my phone rang. The woman on the other end said she found my web-

site on the Internet and started asking what my service was about and
said she would like me to meet with her in about a week and a half to
discuss how my service could benefit her company. (Yes I almost burst
out laughing because I could not believe this was happening.) I was
blown away.

Thanks for giving techniques I would have never thought about to
grow my business.

Tom

Mona owns an upscale formal clothing boutique for women. She used the forgiveness technique even before she attended a workshop for entrepreneurs. Her husband had died and some members of his family were trying to take her assets. She was very worried and her clothing business had suffered as a result. She said that she was in her shop reading an article about forgiveness on my website. She was saying the forgiveness affirmation for her husband's family as a customer walked in. Normally, Mona spends a great deal of time with each customer finding just the right outfit and tailoring it carefully to meet their needs. Suddenly she realized she had been on her computer working on the forgiveness affirmation for five minutes while the customer was in the shop. She apologized to the customer and told her she would be right with her and spend all the time necessary to assist her. The customer smiled and said she had found just what she was looking for. This short time period is a miracle in itself, unheard of for most women shoppers. The customer purchased a dress she had chosen—a designer original, with a high price tag. Mona fully believes it was her forgiveness in action that landed this quick sale. I told her that she holds the record for the fastest manifestation using the forgiveness technique—in only five minutes.

Using the Forgiveness Technique to Assist Clients: For Coaches, Counselors, Therapists and Psychologists

If you are a coach, counselor, therapist or psychologist, this section will be very helpful. If you are a client of one or more of these practitioners you will want to give them a copy of *The Law of Forgiveness* for their personal library.

Life and business coaching has become a business boon. Many satisfied and successful customers attest to the great results they have received. However, the profession of coaching is unregulated at this time, which means literally anyone can hang a shingle and call themselves a coach. Therefore, proper training and discernment become paramount. Coaching is not psychological counseling, nor meant to take its place. This means the assessment process when meeting a new client is essential. If you are a coach and one of your clients has emotional or psychological issues that need professional attention, do not hesitate to refer them immediately to a trusted, competent, holistic licensed mental health practitioner.

Coaching is focused on goal setting and outcomes. Teaching your clients the forgiveness affirmation and the Three-Step Forgiveness Technique for handling a difficult relationship outlined in this book can greatly enhance their success in meeting their goals. In addition, the goal-setting method I teach in my first book, the *Law of Attraction: Develop Irresistible Attraction,* outlines a step-by-step process by which you can develop a strategic plan of action with your clients. You can share some typical results your clients can expect from coaching with this Law of Attraction and Law of Forgiveness method including the following: meeting their life dreams and goals fast, developing and maintaining better relationships, better understanding of their life's purpose, better understanding of their strengths and areas of needed growth, achieving a better life and work balance, and taking their career or business to the next level.

If you are a licensed counselor, psychologist or therapist, etc., the Law of Forgiveness and Law of Attraction techniques I teach can add greatly to your practice. These techniques are very holistic in nature and begin with the premise of viewing the client as "whole." These tools can add a new dimension to your practice when used with clients where appropriate. This is a very positive approach and the clients respond very well. It makes a great compliment to cognitive restructuring of the client's thought processes because of the emphasis on positive self-talk. I have heard from several therapists from different parts of the country who are using these tools with their clients both individually and in group sessions.

The desired overall outcome for both coaching and counseling is to assist clients to experience improved happiness and well-being, which will in turn allow them to live more full lives. Living a more full life includes meeting goals and dreams.

Kate is a Law of Attraction life coach. She attended a two-hour session I presented on using the forgiveness affirmation. She was able to incorporate it into her coaching right away to assist one of her clients with excellent results.

The very next day [after attending the session], I talked with a client who was very angry and feeling powerless about her ex-husband. Her list of grievances was long, including the fact that he had not provided child support in over two years. I immediately thought of the forgiveness affirmation you taught.

My client was really angry and I was hesitant to suggest forgiveness, but I explained to her that it was NOT FOR HIM. As she understood that it was FOR HERSELF and as I shared with her some of the amazing results that your clients and workshop participants have experienced, she agreed to try it. So we said it together several times and she wrote it down. I suggested that she keep repeating it until she was really feeling it.

The next week she reported that it worked! "Out of the blue" he sent her a check for one year's child support and a solid plan to catch up with the balance. Needless to say, she was amazed. And I am so pleased because I now have another powerful tool to offer my clients.

Just like Kate, life coaches, therapists and counselors can really assist their clients by using the forgiveness affirmation.

Using Forgiveness for Health and Healing

My Story of Health and Healing

When I first began studying the Law of Attraction, I was looking for a positive strategy I could use to obtain healing for my own chronic health issues. My doctor told me I had fibromyalgia. For years I had experienced muscle pain all over my body. In my opinion, the word *fibromyalgia* is a description of the symptoms, and not a true diagnosis. *Fibro* means *muscle* and *myalgia* means *pain*. Therefore, fibromyalgia simply means muscle pain. What kind of diagnosis is that? I already knew I had muscle pain.

My Law of Attraction goal wasn't more money, better relationships or a job. My goal was about health and healing. Being a registered nurse, I thought everyone's priority would be their health. I had taught health promotion workshops for years and just assumed everyone was concerned, like me, about obtaining or maintaining good health. I was in for a surprise. Most of my workshop participants listed manifesting more money as their top goal. I thought, well, that's understandable, as most people could use extra income;

health will be their second priority. I was wrong again. The second most popular area for goal setting was relationships. People either wanted a new romantic relationship or wanted to improve a relationship they already had. Surely, health would be the third most popular goal, I thought. I was wrong again. Obtaining a new job, getting a promotion or beginning a new career of their passion was third. Health was a distant fourth area in which people set their goals. As a result, I don't have as many manifestation stories about healing as I do about people receiving money, new and better relationships, and new jobs and careers. However, several people have used the Law of Attraction method I teach, and experienced miracle healings. These are healings that are currently not explained by modern medicine.

However, I do want to make it clear that most people who write an affirmation about health and healing (including myself), are led to the healers who are right for them. Most have not had miracle healings. My story is very interesting in the way it is unfolding at just the right time in history, in a manner that I never expected in a million years.

When I first began teaching the Law of Attraction workshops in 2001, I was so thrilled and amazed with all my workshop participants who were manifesting goals they had been working on for months or years that I placed my healing goal of relieving my years-long struggle with fibromyalgia and other symptoms on the back burner. As a nurse, mother and caregiver, I had developed the habit of placing the needs of others before my own. Also, like many other health care professionals, I had fallen into the trap of providing care for others, but not readily admitting that I needed help and healing myself. In addition, over the years I had started to feel (partly because of interactions with various health practitioners who could never correctly diagnose what was causing my medical problems) that maybe my condition was "all in my head." So, I decided to assist others to reach their goals first, and then I would try to find time to relax at some point and address my own need for healing.

Due to these and other issues, my journey into healing has been lengthy. In the meantime, I have manifested in every other area of my life: I realized more money, improved relationships and advancement in job and career. I'm not sure why my physical healing journey has taken longer. Maybe it's to give others hope that if they never give up, and keep finding and banishing their blocks, their goals will manifest.

I tell my workshop participants that they should not place me on a pedestal because I am still very much on the journey of discovering, learning and healing, just the same as they are. However, I don't believe I have to *arrive* before sharing with others the amazing things I have discovered along the way. As a matter of fact, I don't believe we ever fully arrive; we're always in the process of learning, living and growing. I have learned as much from my workshop participants as they have learned from me.

My Anger Block Removed by Forgiveness

I really thought I had worked through most of my forgiveness issues. However, I know that forgiveness is always a work in progress. Just when I thought I had worked through my forgiveness list, I would remember someone I forgot to forgive, or else I'd find myself angry at someone else. However, I didn't realize I had a huge block that needed forgiveness until I was completing this book.

My husband had a great job when we married. He was a software engineer for a prosperous company; he loved his work, had great benefits and received frequent and substantial raises. He had worked for this company for years and planned to work there until he retired. Then, all of a sudden the company management announced they would begin layoffs. They told their employees that they planned to send computer engineering jobs to India, where salaries were less than half of what they were paying in America. They even had the audacity to fly some workers over from India and have American workers who had been with the company for years train the new workers.

My husband survived many layoffs, but employee morale began to drop with each announcement of a new one. Finally, with the writing on the wall, he volunteered for a layoff and received a nice severance package. By this time the dot.com bubble had burst and computer jobs in America weren't paying what they used to. It took my husband five months to find a new job. When he did, it paid significantly less than the job he had had before the layoffs. I must say that I was quite angry and disillusioned as I watched the middle-class families in the area where we lived experience job cut after job cut. All of us had followed the advice of our parents: We had worked hard in school, received a college education and found a good job with good benefits. We believed we would be set for life. Like my parents' generation we thought that if we were loyal to the company, after thirty years we would enjoy a nice retirement. But with no incentives to keep jobs in the United States, many companies were no longer loyal to the American worker.

In thinking back through my own forgiveness issues, I realized I was still angry about what had happened to my husband and the impact that it had on our family. As I watched the recent news, detailing what was happening to our economy and how hundreds of thousands of people were losing jobs, I knew it was time for forgiveness. I guess I didn't recognize this huge need for forgiveness before, because I wasn't angry with any particular person; instead, I was mad at an entire institution. I was mad at my husband's former company for sending jobs overseas, and I was mad at our government for doing nothing to keep jobs in America. I was mad that this not only negatively impacted our family, but was hurting many hard-working middle-class Americans.

I knew that if I wanted to meet my goal of true health and healing, I needed to forgive sooner, rather than later. I began to forgive Mike's former company, the government, and anyone that I felt might be responsible for what happened to his job. This must have been a huge mountain of energy I moved when I forgave, because two amazing manifestations occurred. The first was for Mike, and the second one was for my healing journey.

Within a few weeks after I forgave my husband's former employer for sending his job overseas and after I forgave our government for not providing any incentives for his company to keep jobs in America, my husband obtained a new job with one of the top thirty software companies in the world. He had wanted to work for this company for many, many years. He had been actively seeking a job there for two years. This company has an average of two to three hundred job applicants for any position they publicly advertise. It is estimated that 25,000 people apply for jobs there each year. The competition was fierce. And they hired Mike. With this new job, he regained most of the income he had lost when his previous job was sent overseas. The company also assured him that he could soon be offered promotions that would allow him to make a salary competitive with the one he had had with his former employer. Needless to say, he was walking on air.

I also experienced an important manifestation for my personal healing. Immediately after forgiving Mike's former employer and the government, I received a referral from my massage therapist to visit a local doctor who ran a pain clinic. When I described my flulike "aching all over" symptoms to the doctor, he ordered some blood tests. When he gave me the results from the blood test, I was absolutely floored. He said that he had ordered a blood test called a Western Blot that checked to see if my body had developed antibodies to Lyme disease. He said the test appeared to be positive for Lyme disease.

For over three decades, I had not had a real diagnosis for what was happening in my body. As I stated before, I only had words that described the symptoms: fibromyalgia, meaning *muscle pain*. Now I had a doctor who had given me a diagnosis.

My pain doctor sent me to a local infectious disease physician who confirmed that I definitely had antibodies to the Lyme bacteria. The standard treatment is a one-month course of antibiotics, but for some people, like me, one month is not enough time to eradicate the Lyme bacteria, which some scientists believe can be what is known as a stealth infection—that is, an infection that can inhabit your body for a long time, can be very difficult to detect and can potentially damage your immune system, cells, tissues and organs. My pain doctor didn't feel comfortable treating me with any additional antibiotics, because other physicians had been harassed by the state medical board for treating patients with this chronic condition. So I manifested a local physician who specializes in integrative medicine to assist me.

Integrative medicine is a combination of traditional Western medicine and natural therapies. I have been seeing this doctor for several months as of this writing, and have been making steady progress. However, being diagnosed with Lyme disease has thrust me into a whole new world of medicine and politics. It is my hope that through my manifestation and healing journey, I can help others who have experienced years of frustration in dealing with a health issue that no one seems to fully understand. The important point to make is that when I fully forgave, I met a goal I had been working on for years. So, if you have forgiven everyone you can think of and still haven't met your goal, dig deeper. Are there people you have forgotten, or organizations, businesses, or governments you still need to forgive? I am living proof that when you forgive completely, manifestations come rushing in.

Forgiving Your Body: The Historic Case of Myrtle Fillmore

In 1886, Myrtle Fillmore, the cofounder of the Unity movement and Silent Unity, an international prayer ministry, was dying of tuberculosis caused by bacteria in a day and age where there was no antibiotic cure. Unlike many young women of her day, Myrtle had delayed marriage and had experienced a successful career as a teacher and founder of her own private school. She had had tuberculosis since she was young, but at the age of forty-three, with two small boys (ages four and two), she found out that she was dying. Her doctors told her they had done all they could to help her. Myrtle turned to her faith to seek healing. She had been a member of the Methodist church for most of her life, and when faced with certain death knocking at her door, she added positive affirmative prayer and healing metaphysics to her belief system. She closed herself in her room and for days, weeks and months, she studied the words of Jesus, concentrating on those that concerned healing. She especially liked the words of Jesus in the Gospel of Mark: "Therefore I tell you, whatever you ask in prayer, believe that you have received it, and it will be yours." In addition to repeating Bible verses, she said positive affirmations about healing. She actually talked to her body, forgiving it and telling her organs they were energetic, strong and intelligent. In his book on Fillmore, Thomas Witherspoon quotes her as saying:

> I went to all the life centers in my body and spoke words of Truth to them—words of strength and power. I asked their forgiveness for the foolish, ignorant course that I had pursued in the past, when I had condemned them and called them weak, inefficient and diseased. I did not become discouraged at their being slow to wake up, but kept right on, both silently and aloud, declaring the words of Truth until the organs responded . . . Then, I asked the Father to forgive me for taking His life into my organism and there using it so meanly. I promised Him that I would never, never again retard the free flow of life through my mind and my body by any false word or thought; that I would always bless it and encourage it with true thoughts and words in its wise work of building up my body temple; that I would use all diligence and wisdom in telling it just what I wanted it to do . . . I did not let any worried or anxious thought into my mind, and I stopped speaking gossipy, frivolous, petulant, angry words.

Around 1888, two years after she began this process, Myrtle was fully healed. This complete healing appeared to be miraculous, as she had been near death from a disease that had no cure until the middle of the next century. Myrtle lived to the ripe old age of 86, and spent the rest of her life developing an international ministry, teaching people how to pray in a positive, affirmative and healing manner.

One hundred and eight years after Myrtle Fillmore was healed, my friend Sharyn experienced a miracle healing using the very same principles.

▓ Forgiving Yourself: Sharyn's Miracle Healing

When I forgave, I was led to the health practitioner who could best help me. However, when my very good friend Sharyn Fuller forgave, she experienced what she calls a *miracle healing*. Her doctors were perplexed, and could not offer a clear or convincing explanation of why, or how, she had healed so fully and quickly. Sharyn had been familiar with the Law of Attraction principles for many years and had used them to meet dreams and goals. But, as we all know, it's sometimes difficult to remember to use the principles during stressful times. Sharyn shares her story in her own words, describing how she lost her way and then got back on track using the Law of Attraction and Law of Forgiveness.

I had been a stay-at-home mom for almost twenty years, and the time had come to go back to work. I had never experienced work more satisfying than that of devoted mother, but my children were almost completely independent, and so I was ready and eager to explore new horizons. Since I am naturally a very outgoing person, love working with people and have always loved looking at houses, I became a residential Realtor and broker in 2005, after taking several required courses and tests.

I have been a believer in the Law of Attraction since I was 18; my belief started in 1974 during a visit to California, at which time I stumbled onto a group of people who exposed me to metaphysics. When I returned to New York I discovered that few people there were aware of that particular philosophy, and when I tried to discuss it I could tell I was labeled as "flaky." So, I began instead to keep metaphysical principles in the back of my mind; I believe I was using metaphysics subconsciously, only pulling the principles up to my active consciousness from time to time, during crisis situations. And sure enough, the next thirty-plus years were thoroughly wonderful and satisfying. I graduated from college, got married and had two beautiful children.

Well, getting back to 2005: During my Realtor training, I read a book that assured me that in order to have a busy enough practice to make a good living it would be necessary to immerse myself in the subject, to live and breathe real estate 24/7. Well, since I was determined to succeed in real estate, and as I felt that I had already succeeded in my other goals, I decided to implement that advice; I started my new career with gusto.

A caring man who was my manager, while pleased with my enthusiasm, cautioned me. He insisted that it was necessary to schedule at least one day a week to relax, and that no one should work 24/7. I did not listen to him, however, and sure enough I had a great first year, doing much better than most new Realtors, selling about $3.5 million worth of residential property.

But in real estate school—perhaps to encourage those who experience the more common slow first year—students are told that agents usually double the first year's income in the second year. So, because of that alleged truism—my mind and heart would accept nothing less! And unfortunately, while I seemed to be on track to accomplish this in the first part of the year, several problems that were out of my control arose during the second half of the year that put my goal into serious jeopardy. Instead of maintaining my optimism (as I usually managed to do), and keeping everything in perspective, fear of failure took over and began to cause me great stress. I decided that if I could not reach my goal during that second year I would be humiliated, and with that thought in mind I generated STRESS instead of effective energy. This, of course, snowballed negatively, and affected not only my career but my marriage.

While my marriage to Larry was in its twenty-third year and had always been strong, it began to suffer from the strain of my negative thinking. As my second year as a Realtor progressed and it looked less and less like I was going to double my first year's output, I placed more and more pressure on myself; and I put even less time into my relationships with my family members, particularly my husband.

Instead of ever taking time off to relax, instead of enjoying the present and my many blessings, instead of remembering the fact that not everything can be controlled, I began to berate myself when business deals went wrong, and I felt pessimistic about the future. It is impossible to enjoy the present when one becomes consumed with negative thoughts, and those thoughts always generate anxiety. I had forgotten the Law of Attraction principle that tells us that what we focus on grows. This means that by focusing on frustrations with my business, I was actually attracting more of the same. I was actually blocking my goals from manifesting, because of my negative feelings and thoughts.

August of 2006 arrived, and I found myself more than halfway through the year, but not nearly halfway to my lofty expectations. I became even more consumed with self-anger and condemnation, which did not feel good at all. For the first time in my life, doctors began recommending blood pressure–lowering medications—which I refused to take, since I knew the cause of my soaring pressure was my thwarted ambitions, and the high blood pressure would go away as soon as my business was on track. But since I finally got to the point where I felt just terrible all the time, I decided I had to do something relaxing, even if it meant taking time off. So my husband and I made plans to enjoy a relaxing weekend at the North Carolina coast.

It was the last Saturday in August and we were at a resort. We had just spent the day on the beach, though the truth was I had actually spent most of it *trying* to relax. Who knew that relaxing could take so much effort?

In the elevator, on the way down to an elegant dinner with my husband, a severe wave of dizziness hit me. No longer able to stand, to my husband's surprise I suddenly slumped to the floor. The doors of the elevator opened, my husband looked down at me, puzzled, and said, "Okay, honey, stop kidding around and please get up—we're here!"

I tried to get up, but for some reason my head was spinning and my heart was pounding, and I was completely unable to do so.

I had no idea what was going on, but my first rationalization was that perhaps—having eaten so little during the day due to anxiety—I was experiencing a sudden drop in blood sugar, and that maybe I had hypoglycemia, a condition I had always heard about. So I thought if Larry could help me over to the restaurant and I could get some sugar into my bloodstream, the dizziness would abate.

Shortly after we sat down, I ate some creamy crab soup. Well, much to my horror and dismay it immediately erupted back out of my body like a volcano . . . and then adding to that humiliation was a sudden excruciating pain that felt like my head was exploding.

My husband took me back to our room. Now I was convinced that my weird problems were all just due to having the worst migraine in the world, perhaps coupled with an inner ear infection (which is known to affect balance—and, after all, I had been swimming), so I was determined to grin and bear it as I did with everything else. And I withstood it for two days, lying in bed with all the lights off. Unable to take pain meds since the nausea was so intense that I could not keep even a sip of water down, I suffered without food or water in constant agony (unable to even open my eyes due to the pain and dizziness) for two whole days. On the third day of my agony, I finally got to a doctor, who immediately sent me to an emergency room. Once there, a brain scan indicated I had suffered a stroke.

A stroke? That couldn't happen to me! I didn't have any known risk factors for having a stroke. I was not overweight, was below the age of fifty-five, I exercised regularly, had low cholesterol, (usually) had low blood pressure, did not have diabetes and there was no history of stroke in my family.

When told the diagnosis, my poor husband was devastated. But after the initial shock and surprise, I had a totally different reaction—I wanted to weep with relief! Because now that I had a serious diagnosis, I could justifiably relax! Not only that, I was finally in a place that would make the pain go away. (Or so I thought at the time.)

I was immediately admitted to the hospital, and the hospital staff tried one thing after another (intravenously) to relieve my head pain. But nothing they did even slightly reduced the feeling that my skull was exploding, much less brought back my equilibrium.

For five days straight I could not walk, sit up, or even focus my eyes on anything. I could barely even talk coherently—my sentences seemed to trail off into nothingness. However, despite the pain and nausea, I remember thoroughly enjoying myself compared to how I had been feeling prior to the hospitalization. I began to enjoy being taken care of around the clock, to enjoy the concern and the attention, and most importantly, I was finally able to let go of the self-imposed demands. I was able to forgive myself for not meeting my sales goals, and could allow my body to have proper rest and relaxation. Not only that, but I became totally aware of my husband's unwavering love and support, and I felt so lucky, and optimistic that all would be well.

My poor husband, however, was extremely distraught. On the second day of my hospital stay, an MRI (a test that shows layers of the brain) was done on my brain—and it looked ominous. It showed a big black cloud over two-thirds of my cerebellum; this was interpreted as dead and/or dying brain cells, indicating permanent brain damage. Three doctors conferred; they couldn't decide what had caused the damage, and because of my lack of risk factors, they were considering the possibility that the cloud was hiding a fast-growing brain tumor, and so a brain biopsy was suggested.

One doctor decided to be blunt about what all three were thinking and told my husband that I clearly had permanent brain damage. He stated emphatically that we had to accept the fact I would never walk again. He even gave Larry a list of nursing homes to start calling because I would need 24/7 care for at least six months. He said that perhaps if I had intense physical therapy during that time, I might, at best, learn to walk with a walker!

This was a Wednesday afternoon, almost five days after the stroke. Larry was consulting with the doctor in the hallway, and when he came back into my room, I asked him what the doctor had said. But all he told me was that I might need a brain biopsy sometime soon, because they weren't sure if I had a stroke or a little brain tumor, but either way I would be fine.

He didn't sound worried, so I continued to enjoy my mental and emotional escape, despite the constant pain and nausea. Then I remembered that I had plans with my friend Connie Domino. I had Larry dial her number for me, and after leaving a long, rambling message on her voice mail, I went back to feeling so grateful for my husband's constant reassuring presence by my side. In the meantime Larry barely ate, accompanied me to every test, and stayed all night long in a chair by my bed. Despite the extreme physical discomfort I actually was enjoying the wonderful attention of Larry, the concerned phone calls from friends and family, and the attentive care of all the doctors, nurses and technicians.

Later on Wednesday I had a visitor—my good friend Connie. I was wearing a sleep mask (donned Saturday night when the head pain had set in, as removing all vestiges of light helped a tiny bit) so while I could not see her, I knew it was Connie as soon as I heard her distinctive voice.

I can't say I remember much of anything in detail, but I do remember being further assured that all would be well. And then, apparently after noticing the grim look on my husband's grim face, she, too, had a consultation with him in the hallway—only hers was more of the optimistic kind! From what Connie and Larry have told me, the conversation went something like this:

"Larry, I know she looks bad, I know what the doctor says, but miracles happen all the time! Okay, not often, but I'm a nurse and I've seen it all. And if anyone could pull off a miracle, it's Sharyn! She is tenacious, and that's what it takes, so don't lose heart! Just don't tell her what the doctor says, don't let her spirits go down, and keep visualizing her well and healthy. Just keep seeing her in perfect health again, and trust me, despite what they say, it can come true. Don't lose hope!"

And my husband did just as Connie insisted, despite his fears. He threw that list of nursing homes into the trash can determined to never need it, determined that he would take care of me 24/7 himself if necessary.

A tray of dinner food came and went, me unable to eat a thing. It got late, and Larry pulled up a chair to sleep as close as he could to me. I tried hard to ignore the pain and sleep too, and with all the drugs that were pumping ineffectively through my IV, I believe I did doze a little. In my drug-induced stupor I felt no fear, and even through the pain and even in my sleep I continued to enjoy the surrender, the release of the increasing pressure and negative self-talk that I'd experienced over the past eight months. Despite the circumstances, I was able to let it all drain out of me.

Following Connie's advice, Larry visualized me well and healthy, touching his head to mine, imagining the pain draining out into his own head, picturing me well and healthy. Eventually he, too, dozed. At 4:30 a.m. on Thursday, a technician came into my room to take my vital signs. And after almost five days of complete incapacity, when the technician came to my bed, I sat up. And at that moment I realized the pain was gone. I realized I felt just fine.

Larry became aware that I could sit up, that the pain in my head was gone, and that I was asking to check my e-mail. He was delirious with joy. A miracle had actually happened.

A few hours later, the doctor who had said that I would never walk again came into my room. I was sitting up in bed, working on my laptop, happily going through all my piled up e-mails. He was astonished.

First they wanted to know what caused the MRI to look so ominous and after having a special test to examine the heart, called an echocardiogram, the congenital (present at birth) hole in my heart was discovered and the doctors deduced it had allowed a blood clot to go through to my brain. It had made its way into my cerebellum, causing that part of my brain to malfunction. The cerebellum controls our equilibrium, an extremely important function, allowing us to precieve our body's position in space. It is the equilibrium that allows us to maintain our balance. With my equilibrium not functioning, it suddenly felt like my whole body was on an out-of-control carnival ride, causing instant and extreme nausea.

I've since had that hole closed, so it can never happen again. But what caused my equilibrium to come back when the MRI made that look hopeless? What made the pain go away? A subsequent MRI looked very similar, and when I questioned that brain surgeon he said he didn't really know, but the important thing was that I was fine now, so it mattered not a whit what the MRI showed.

It will probably always remain a mystery. But what I think is that I had begun making unrealistic demands of myself, and that I wasn't cutting myself any slack. And when you think unhealthy thoughts, your body will eventually rebel. Once I let go of all of the demands, when I forgave myself for not achieving my career goals immediately and for not being as perfect as I demanded myself to be, when I finally surrendered to all the love and happiness that was around me—but that I was ignoring—my health came back.

I left the hospital on Friday, seven days after my stroke, and came home to a house that looked like a greenhouse. My house was full of plants, flowers, food and gifts from friends, coworkers, family members and neighbors, causing my spirits to soar even higher. It made me even more aware of how loved I was, which was so much more important than career goals. In addition, my husband insisted that I take the rest of the year off, so that I could totally rest and really garner up my strength. What a blessing that was, and it was especially loving, since it was from the man who had dreamed of retiring soon due to my sudden rise in my real estate career; this decision meant that he had to continue working for a much longer time.

During my extended—and very relaxing—vacation, I visited the set of a shoot for the HGTV real estate reality show *Buy Me*. Feeling quite exuberant, I chatted with the film crew, giving them my card (not mentioning my stroke). A month after that—now January 2007—I went back to my real estate office, wondering how I was going to garner the necessary enthusiasm to get back into finding clients for real estate after such an enjoyable hiatus. Sure enough, on my answering machine was a message from the *Buy Me* producer in Montreal, Canada. She said they were looking for outgoing real estate agents in the Raleigh area who would like to have the sale of one of their listings filmed for a reality show and would I be interested in doing a show? Suddenly, all of my enthusiasm came rushing back like a train! Through remaining relaxed and positive, I was able to manifest a dream—having my real estate career highlighted on a nationally televised show.

Eventually, I filmed not one but *two* episodes for the nine-show series, both of which have since been shown numerous times on HGTV and continue to be shown to this day. Since *Buy Me* is a reality show, not all stories end happily—but both of mine were so positive that they have been wonderful advertising for me, causing my real estate career to blossom again!

The national *Realtor Magazine* even did a "Success Story" about me in their July 2008 issue. So life continues to be good, and I continue to be blessed.

But only when I don't forget the principles that Connie teaches!

Part of healing involves forgiving those who we perceived to have wronged us even when that person is you. When forgiveness, faith, belief, thought and energy come together, miracles can follow.

Mad at the World: Using Forgiveness to Reach a Higher Consciousness and Live Your Best Life

Thank Goodness You're Starting at the Top

There's been lots of grumbling lately. The twenty-four-hour news-people who talk to us from the TV tell us that things just aren't right. They tell us we should be mad at someone, but most of them can't figure out just who that someone should be. First they tell us we're losing our jobs in record numbers and then they tell us we are the proud owners of things we didn't even know we purchased—big things—like banks, insurance companies and car manufacturers. Some of us want to know if we now own all these big companies, where are our CEO checks, bonus money, mansions and private air-planes. We were beginning to think CEO means "Carted Everyone's money Offshore." We are frustrated because we see people we elected to high office engaging in questionable practices and not being held accountable. We begin to wonder if there truly are people who are above the law. We know we're not above the law because when we get caught speeding, we have to go to traffic court, and we figure if we got caught doing anything more than speeding, we'd be held accountable for that, too.

Yes, we hear lots of complaints about modern society. Some people long for the "good ol' days"—the days way back when life was glorious and people behaved themselves. However, when we closely study written history, we find there really were no good ol' days. Lots of bad things were happening to good people at any given time throughout history. There just weren't as many people recording it or taking notice because the average person was expending so much time trying to place a meal on the table and a roof over their heads. The literate people who were recording history were often members of the aristocracy and were biased in their reporting.

Indeed, we are some of the most fortunate people in the world in that we are blessed to live in the top two levels of Maslow's hierarchy of needs. This hierarchy was a model developed by Abraham Maslow, using five levels that perfectly explain how a person is expending energy, and how his or her efforts depend on current circumstances. At the bottom of the hierarchy, we find those things that our bodies absolutely need to survive: fluids and food. On the next level, we find safety and shelter. If our basic physical needs are met, in that we have fluids, food, safety and shelter, we have the time and energy to move up to the top three levels, which are psychosocial in nature. The third level is love and belonging. In this level, we think about those we love, and those we desire to spend time with. We establish relationships of various types; we may join a supportive group of friends and a community of caring. The fourth level addresses our self-esteem.

In addition to the psychosocial need of love and belonging, we also may seek status, success and prestige through our education, career and/or relationships. The very top level is self-actualization. In this level, people seek to improve their lives by engaging in formal and informal study, furthering their career, obtaining a better job, beginning a business or a new hobby.

For much of written history, large numbers of people spent the majority of their time and energy on the bottom two levels of the hierarchy of needs, trying every day to obtain enough food and clean water to survive, and securing shelter and safety. When a person's energy is tied up in these first two levels, there isn't much time to spend on thinking about loving others, how we feel about ourselves, and furthering one's career.

What makes our society unique is that for the first time in written history, large groups of people have the privilege and pleasure of spending the vast majority of their time in the top three tiers of the hierarchy of needs: searching for love and belonging, self-esteem, and working on self-actualization. Yet it seems as a whole, we are complaining more.

I definitely don't think things are worse today. I think we simply have the luxury of having the time to complain. And we also have the ability to know about everyone's misfortune. The information age and communication explosion have increased the speed with which communication is sent and received by leaps and bounds. Greater numbers of people are educated and literate. In addition, people everywhere are inclined to take pictures, record digital images, and send text messages, often using a mobile phone that can be carried anywhere. The likelihood that negative incidents will be recorded and sent across the globe, via the Internet, is greatly increased. This proliferation of negative images certainly gives the impression that more bad things are happening, but this really doesn't stand the test of time.

I fully believe we will repeat (and in parts of the world we are already repeating) the less savory aspects of history if we don't study and understand them and actively seek to create new paradigms for interacting with one another. Becoming aware of how fortunate we are, developing an attitude of gratitude, and engaging in the for- giveness affirmation technique anytime we feel wronged are the first important steps in the direction of living in harmony with ourselves and others in our world.

Justice and the Forgiveness Technique

One of the most fascinating things I have learned about activating the Law of Forgiveness is that moving energy using forgiveness can expedite the Law of Justice and Order.

I had a Law of Attraction workshop participant who had a goal of meeting her ideal partner. She had had a very bad marriage in her past, and before the workshop began, she said that she didn't think she would ever meet a man who would treat her well. In her goal affirmation she listed the attributes she desired in a partner, and lo and behold, this very man came into her life two weeks later. Several months later they were married.

I saw her a year later and she told me about the other goal she had manifested during the last year. Her ex-husband had molested all five of her children. For eleven years she had been trying to bring this man to justice with no success. It's hard to imagine the inten- sity of the anger and resentment she felt. Forgiving him was a dif- ficult decision for her, but she decided it was time to release and move on. When she sincerely said the forgiveness affirmation for her ex-husband, the wheels of justice began to move and he was placed in prison. This may seem confusing because when you forgive someone, you aren't asking for any specific fate for this person. You are not including any thoughts of malice in your forgiveness, or the energy wouldn't move. You're actually releasing the person who has offended you, and the energy that is tied up between the two of you. However, what I have discovered from my Law of Attraction and Law of Forgiveness students is that when you release the energy, whatever justice that is supposed to happen, moves into place.

Another Law of Attraction and Law of Forgiveness student was angry that a commercial product she had invented had been stolen from her by the very people who had made a commitment to help her market it. She had trusted these people. The product was successfully marketed and made 4.2 million dollars. She took her case to court, but she lost the case. She believes that the people who stole her product had paid off a corrupt judge for $30,000 to rule in their favor. She was filled with anger and resentment. Her thoughts were very negative, and a multitude of bad things happened in her life. She went bankrupt, lost her job, moved into a mobile home, an opossum died under her mobile home, black flies filled her mobile home, her purse was stolen and her car was damaged by a hit-and-run driver. Phew! Nothing was going her way!

After she sincerely said the forgiveness affirmation for the people who stole her product, and for the dishonest judge, the authorities arrested the judge, who is being charged with taking bribes in other cases. Her case is now being reconsidered.

One of my first Law of Attraction students said the forgiveness affirmation and one week later she received a check in the mail for $25,000, for a ten-year-old lawsuit that was suddenly settled.

A significant number of my students who are going through a divorce tell me that after saying the forgiveness affirmation for their former spouse, things proceeded much more smoothly and it was much easier to obtain what they wanted in the divorce settlement.

I have learned so much from my workshop participants, coaching clients and readers about all the amazing properties of the Law of Forgiveness. It works in ways that I would not have guessed. As we learn more and more about this incredible universal law, we may totally change how we consider the topic of justice. My guess is we will finally come to understand that resorting to violence and/or revenge to obtain justice is both counterproductive and completely unnecessary. If an individual forgiving their aggressor can clear the way for the wheels of justice to move, just imagine what would happen if the entire country or the entire world forgives. My guess is the light would shine on all that is corrupt and hiding in the shadows and the truth will be made known to all.

Amish Grace: Forgiveness, Justice and Pardon

When the topic of forgiveness and justice is discussed, sooner or later the Amish—and their unique understanding and practice—enter the conversation. The Amish approach to forgiveness became a national topic for discussion several years ago when tragedy struck their community. On October 2, 2006, a gunman named Charles Carl Roberts IV entered an Amish schoolhouse near Nickel Mines, Pennsylvania. Five schoolgirls were killed, and five others were seriously injured. Then Roberts killed himself. The world wasn't as shocked by the school shooting in the quiet Amish countryside as it was by the response of the Amish community. Almost immediately the Amish of Nickel Mines forgave the killer and offered support to his family. The evening after the killing, several members of a nearby Amish community visited Roberts's widow, Amy, and her children; several miles away, another member visited the killer's father. When Roberts was buried several days later, more than half of those attending the funeral were Amish. The parents of several of the slain students extended an invitation to the Roberts family to attend their daughters' funerals.

Those who study Amish culture were not surprised by this response. Donald Kraybill, Steven Holt and David Weaver-Zercher wrote in their book, *Amish Grace*:

> When forgiveness arrived at the killer's home within hours of his crime, it did not appear out of nowhere. Rather, forgiveness is woven into the very fabric of Amish life, its sturdy threads having been spun from faith in God, scriptural mandates, and a history of persecution.

To better understand how the Amish can forgive so easily under horrific circumstances, we must briefly examine their history. The Amish came to America in the 1700s and 1800s, settling in Pennsylvania, Ohio, Indiana and eventually other states. Like other early immigrants, they were searching for religious freedom. The movement formed in Europe during the early 1500s at the time of the Protestant Reformation. Due to their belief in adult baptism, at first the Amish were called Anabaptists, which meant *rebaptizers*. They also believed in separation of church and state. Both of these beliefs infuriated Catholic and Protestant state-sanctioned churches who considered infant baptism to be sufficient. As a result, many Anabaptists were severely persecuted, often burned at the stake or decapitated. Anabaptists believe in a literal interpretation of the Bible and place special emphasis on the teachings of Jesus, especially the Sermon on the Mount where Jesus talks about forgiveness. They believe that God can only forgive them if they forgive others. Their beliefs regarding forgiveness stem mostly from verses in the New Testament and especially the Lord's Prayer, where Jesus said, "Forgive us our debts as we forgive our debtors."

The Amish views on forgiveness extend to their beliefs regarding personal and national defense. The Amish are conscientious objectors to military service. They don't believe in any act that may be considered to be revenge, including fighting in a war or bringing suit against another person in court. The Amish belief in unconditional forgiveness is truly amazing. They suffer the same problems that plague any other society—death, illness, violence, abuse, etc.—and yet, they always have forgiveness in their hearts. Kraybill and his colleagues end their book, *Amish Grace*, with this thought:

> In a world where faith often justifies and magnifies revenge, and in a nation where some Christians use scripture to fuel retaliation, the Amish response was indeed a surprise. Regardless of the details of the Nickel Mines story, one message rings clear: religion was used not to justify rage and revenge but to inspire goodness, forgiveness, and grace. And that is the big lesson for the rest of us regardless of our faith or nationality.

Three Stages of Spiritual or Psychological Development

When people begin the journey to forgiveness, and experience their true spiritual power, they enter a new state of being. This surprises many people and they express awe at the speed of their spiritual and emotional growth. They ask me to explain what in the world has just happened to them. Quite simply they have advanced from the *To Me* stage of spiritual or psychological development to the *Through Me* stage. This is no small occurrence as most of the people in the world today spend their entire lives in the *To Me* stage. Let me explain.

Several years ago, I attended a presentation given by a minister named Sky St. John. According to Sky, there are three spiritual or psychological developmental stages people can experience. These stages are *To Me, Through Me* and *Just Be*. My work with the Law of Forgiveness and the Law of Attraction takes us from the stage of "things are happening *To Me*," to the stage of "things are happening *Through Me*."

In the *To Me* stage, people feel they have very little power over their life. They feel they are a victim of circumstances. If bad things happen to them, they're sure they're having a run of bad luck, or if they're miserable, maybe it's God's will. Sometimes they blame others—perhaps their spouse or children, a boss, the whole of society or even God—for their problems. Others may hate themselves. In the *To Me* stage, many believe there is not enough abundance in the universe, and they must rush in to get their share, before someone else steals their chance. They may believe in revenge. They may truly feel that it's a dog eat dog world, life's not fair, and then you die. They often believe that to forgive is a sign of weakness and is an admission that the person who hurt them was correct in their actions.

Unfortunately, many of the citizens in our world live in the *To Me* stage. Therefore, you can imagine when someone presents a message of hope, like that offered by the Law of Forgiveness, people become excited. It sounds "old hat" to those of us who have been studying these principles for years, but it can be music to the ears of those who haven't. Just like the Law of Attraction, the Law of Forgiveness takes those willing to learn and practice it from the *To Me* stage of spiritual development to the *Through Me* stage.

When people realize life events are happening *through* them, not *to* them, they understand they have created their own reality and can take responsibility for it. They lose their victim mentality. It is also at this stage that people learn they have the power within them to manifest abundance in their lives. They become as excited as children with their newly discovered abilities, and are eager to manifest their goals and dreams. Once a person comes to the understanding that they have control over their life and circumstances by abiding by positive spiritual principles and universal laws, they are not so frightened anymore. At this point, they can begin to envision a world where people can best obtain success and happiness by assisting others to do the same.

Once a critical mass of people has entered the *Through Me* stage of spiritual development, I believe the whole world will change. They will realize that there is enough—and more than enough—for everyone. There will be no need for violence and war because they will realize *there is enough abundance for everyone*—and the well never runs dry. They will realize their goals and dreams through their own creative process, making it unnecessary to obtain what they want by force. They won't feel compelled to take what they want from other people or strip nature bare before, as they fear, time runs out on their chance. Living by the principle that *there is more than enough* will allow them to relax, and come to a place of peace and harmony with themselves, as well as with others around them, and with nature itself.

Many people will choose to remain in the *Through Me* stage, and that's okay. World peace can actually be accomplished if enough people reach this place of understanding. Believe it or not, we don't have to all be in the *Just Be* stage for the world to live in harmony.

However, those who choose to do so can proceed to the stage in which it's enough to *Just Be*. This is the stage of the master teacher. It's a wonderful place of spiritual and psychological development, but can easily be misunderstood. Some people believe it's the only stage of worth, and those who reach it have given up worldly comforts to live an ascetic lifestyle. In actuality, those who *fully* enter this stage can literally manifest everything they need and desire as they go along. They no longer have the need to manifest a great amount of "stuff." They already know (and many have proven) that they can do that if they so choose. They realize by this time that they desire simplicity—simple, natural and spiritual comforts—more than anything else. They place a premium on remaining in balance with nature and all that surrounds them.

Several years ago, I attended a talk given by a minister, Reverend Neusom Holmes, about a man who wanted to see if he could prove this principle. Neusom told the story of Jeffrey Sawyer from Asheville, North Carolina, who quit his job, sold all his belongings and set out on a walking journey to inquire into the meaning of life, love and freedom. He had no particular destination in mind, and hiked 3,500 miles over several years with only basic necessities—a few clothes, a blanket, a mosquito net, matches and a little flour and salt. He carried no ATM card, no credit card and no tent. Jeffrey Sawyer manifested his needs as he traveled. If people gave him money, he often gave it away at the end of the day. By creating a sincere vacuum, his well never ran dry. This doesn't mean he had an easy trip. He often struggled to understand the difference between what he "needed" to survive and what he "desired." He focused on making sure *he didn't come from a place of need,* but instead a place of perceived *abundance.* He wasn't begging for provisions. He was kind and emotionally supportive to those he met, therefore, giving as he received. Jeffrey wanted to understand whether he owned money or money owned him, and eventually came to the conclusion that only by giving up "the psychological hold on what we think is ours" can we "see the bounty all around us."

By the end of the trip Jeffrey Sawyer felt like one of the most prosperous people in the world.

Jesus, and other divine leaders and master teachers, lived their lives in the *Just Be* stage. This doesn't mean they were poor. They literally manifested everything they needed and desired daily. They always had food, shelter and clothing when they wanted it. A surprising number of people believe that most master teachers wore rags. Jesus did not wear rags; in fact, his robe was so nice that Roman soldiers threw dice for it after the crucifixion. A friend, Joseph of Arimathea, insisted on contributing his own unused tomb, where the body of Jesus was laid, having been prepared with precious spices and fine linen. When food or wine was needed by his friends, Jesus manifested it.

As stated before, the majority of people are still very much in the *To Me* stage of existence. They believe they are victims of circumstance. They believe there is *not enough* and they must *get their fair share* before someone else steals it from them. This false belief system has led many people to lead quiet (and sometimes not-so-quiet) lives of desperation. It has led to wars, more wars and rumors of wars.

In order to truly change the world for the good of all, people must first experience for themselves their own positive spiritual power. They must have viable proof there are predictable, unchanging universal laws and principles that they can tap into to manifest good and abundance in their lives.

Due to centuries of negative training, most people in what we call the developed, or industrialized, countries must experience the *Through Me* stage before proceeding to the *Just Be* stage. Going from Point A (*To Me*) to Point C (*Just Be*), without experiencing Point B (*Through Me*) is a leap of faith too large for their comfort level. Just like the Law of Attraction, what is unearthed in the Law of Forgiveness is a technique to help people quickly move from the *To Me* to the *Through Me* stage. When they apply the formula I teach, they can meet their goals and dreams very quickly, sometimes in less than two weeks. Some readers and participants have actually had significant results in less than twenty-four hours. At this point, they have viable proof they can manifest all they need through the power found within themselves.

After proving that these principles—the Law of Attraction and the Law of Forgiveness—work at a personal level, and can enhance their own lives, they will have the assurance and confidence needed to share these principles with the rest of the world.

The Big Picture: From Personal Forgiveness to World Peace

Let's Start a Revolution

Forgiveness and reconciliation are not just ethereal, spiritual, other-worldly activities. They have to do with the real world. They are real-politik, because in a very real sense, without forgiveness, there is no future. —Archbishop Desmond Tutu

I was a big fan of Ann Landers, who had a syndicated advice column in the daily newspaper for many years. I couldn't wait to turn to the Life Section of our newspaper and read the practical advice that Ann doled out every day. I also appreciated the fact that when she made mistakes or gave bad advice, she willingly admitted it and apologized. What I most enjoyed was Ann's Forgiveness Day. Each year, she would declare a Day of Forgiveness when all readers were encouraged to forgive someone they held a grudge against. Ann didn't even explain how they should forgive, just requested they do it. I could hardly believe the letters that poured in afterward. The healing of people, families and broken relationships was incredible. When Ann simply declared one day a year for forgiveness, she touched a multitude of lives in an incredibly profound way.

I began to wonder what it would be like if the whole world were to declare one day a year to be a Day of Forgiveness. What an impact that one day would make! It would be mind boggling. I was so excited about how personal forgiveness can assist people at a personal level; I wondered how this could change our nation and our world.

After receiving story after story of how the forgiveness technique I teach moved energy quickly and changed lives forever, I decided to develop a gigantic Law of Attraction goal—a super-large goal, if you will. I've always been the rebellious type, so the thought of starting a revolution appealed to me. All the passion, the excitement, the energy movement that a true uprising could bring really motivated me to action. But would a revolution be a good thing? I am a history buff and know the word *revolution* hasn't always had the most positive connotation. Many revolts down through history, at some point became—shall we say—somewhat *ugly*. So, I turned to my good friend, *Merriam-Webster's Collegiate Dictionary*, to assist me in deciphering this dilemma. Merriam defines a revolution as "a fundamental change in the way of thinking about or visualizing something: a change in paradigm." I liked this definition. An upheaval doesn't have to be difficult, negative or brutal. I realized that it is high time large groups of people experience a *positive revolution*.

And what could be more positive than a Forgiveness Revolution? It was something people really needed; something important; something peaceful that people could approach with passion; something that could help them meet their life's dreams and goals rapidly; and something that could positively change lives profoundly, quickly, and forever. I knew from all the success stories and case studies pouring in that forgiveness moves energy faster than any other of my tools. When the specific technique I teach is enacted sincerely, positive results generally happen "out of the blue" within a week or less, and are often no less than miraculous.

Therefore, I affirm the beginning of a Revolution—*A Revolution in Forgiveness*. The ideas, principles and guidelines presented in this book can create a paradigm shift.

Stephen Covey, in *The 7 Habits of Highly Effective People* describes a paradigm as, "the way we see the world—not in terms of our visual sense of sight, but in terms of perceiving, understanding, and interpreting." The shift I'm describing is so powerful, so unprecedented on a large scale, it will completely change the way you and many others reach your dreams and goals—fast.

As we have discussed thus far, the forgiveness technique I teach allows for the release and movement of energy, without the need for batteries, bells, buttons, boxes or buzzers. Therefore, it can be described as a type of cutting edge *social* or *spiritual technology*. It is voice- or thought-activated by you, through your sincerity, intention, will and action. You are about to be introduced to the *ripple* or *domino effect* since this energy travels instantly. This means even though you're just one person, you can make a huge impact on others. This can include your family, social network, community, and yes, even the world, through activating the enormous untapped power found in this technique.

Today, I am extending to you a personal invitation to join the Forgiveness Revolution. It's the hottest, most powerful movement happening in our world. It is taking place right here and right now, and you mustn't miss a minute before becoming involved.

How Do You Join the Forgiveness Revolution?

First, you make a decision to join, and then you do it.

Second, you read, and practice the principles of forgiveness and the affirmation technique found in Chapter 2. Then, if you so choose, you invite others to do the same. You can find more information at: *www .JointheForgivenessRevolution.com* or *www.TheLawofForgiveness.com*.

It is my highest aim to bring about a fundamental change in the way people have traditionally thought about, understood and practiced forgiveness. This change has enormous potential to lead to

Membership in the Forgiveness Revolution

Our Mission: We have met our positive goals and bettered our own lives, family, community, country and world through understanding and applying the social and spiritual technology of forgiveness.

We accept everyone; we embrace diversity. The business of forgiveness is equal opportunity; everyone is invited to join in.

We seek to enrich the lives of everyone who hears the call to forgive.

Each act of forgiveness will be begun by a personal decision in the heart of the one wishing to be free from the tyranny of anger, resentment and fear.

There is no membership hierarchy for all are equal in their desire for healing and wholeness without boundaries or limitations.

Members shall recognize one another by the love in their hearts, their desire for healing and wholeness, and the outcome of their actions.

Each member shall seek to advance the Revolution of Forgiveness by actively practicing the forgiveness technique and, as they are ready, leading and teaching by example.

Members are joyful and on the journey to transcend doubt and fear— for their work is great and their witness prevails.

positive personal empowerment and successful results like the world has never seen before. *The revolution is on!*

The Big Picture: Forgiveness and Future Generations

Forgiveness has been talked about for years, and many books have been written on the subject. Why should we begin an entire revolution dedicated to forgiveness? If you ask them, most people will include somewhere in their explanation the importance of forgiving each other, and saving the world for future generations. What about saving future generations *now*?

Some people may find it surprising that according to the Centers for Disease Control, after accidents, homicide and suicide are the most common causes of death in adolescents and young adults in America. Let me repeat this fact, as it is almost unbelievable: After accidents, the majority of American youth die through being murdered, either by someone else, or by their own hand. This is completely unacceptable for a civilized society. It does tell us that we're doing a pretty good job of controlling childhood diseases, which used to be the highest cause of mortality among young people in the past. However, it also tells us that new strategies are needed to address the emotional distress faced by today's youth. We need to teach young people about the forgiveness affirmation technique now more than ever before, to give them a positive alternative to violence and revenge.

From the time they are small, our children are taught through movies, television and popular video games that violence and revenge are acceptable methods for handling anger and frustration. Entire movie plots and video game strategies are developed in which seeking revenge is used as the primary method for righting wrongs. The nation was shocked recently when several children in third grade were arrested at school for carrying weapons they intended to use to kill their teacher—but should we really be that surprised?

When we closely examine gang violence and terrorism, we find shocking similarities. Many people believe that gangs and terrorist groups form based primarily on adherence to a certain religion, philosophy or lifestyle. However, when we cut through the hype what we really find is that both the gangs in our country and terrorist organizations here and abroad are largely formed by disaffected young men who do not have regular jobs and do not feel they can obtain success through the normal mechanisms offered by their society. Young men who cannot find legal employment earning enough money to support a middle-class lifestyle make perfect recruits for gangs and terrorist groups. While these groups are small in numbers when compared with the greater population, the terrorism and violence they have wrought has caused such fear and reaction that it has been devastating for our country and others. Most people will agree that we need to do something. The old adage that an ounce of prevention is worth a pound of cure is certainly applicable to this problem.

Reaching out to our young men with a message of hope and a strategy of forgiveness can make a huge difference in their outlook as well as their future. When even one young man is saved from a life of anger and acting out, our whole society moves toward becoming a safer place.

Many people still believe the answer is more prisons, more bombs and increased destruction. In the United States, we currently have more people in prison than any other country in the world. More African-American men are in our prison system than are coming into our university system for their first year. We certainly have more bombs and a larger arsenal containing weapons of mass destruction than most other countries. Are we now going to build even more prisons to house our third-graders who bring weapons to school? Where will it all end? Perhaps it's time to consider other strategies.

What if we took even a fraction of the money spent on war, and used it to ensure that the young people of our country, and the countries with terrorists, were properly nurtured with adult mentors, educated and employed? What if we taught people that forgiveness as a strategy has *power* in it to make their dreams come true? What if we begin to teach the true meaning of the Law of Liberty, which teaches that the only true way I can protect my rights and freedom is to protect yours even if I don't like you, don't agree with you and think you're going to hell in a hand basket? What if we teach people that if I destroy your freedom and take away your rights, ultimately I destroy my own? Out of self-interest, once people understand how universal principles work, more and more people will be motivated to forgive, and to protect and ensure the rights of others.

A Past Model for Reaching World Peace and Reconciliation Through Forgiveness: Nelson Mandela, Desmond Tutu and the End of Apartheid

With the advent of the Internet and instantaneous communication, strategies for peacemaking are changing. Add to that an increased understanding of quantum physics, and a better understanding of the laws that govern the holographic universe, and the future appears filled with exciting possibilities. Before we study how peacemaking may be accomplished in the future, it is important to review the past, and examine some of the best examples of peaceful peacemaking that have involved forgiveness as a strategy.

With much of history filled with wars, more wars and rumors of wars, it is difficult to believe that peace and reconciliation can be achieved through forgiveness. It stretches the imagination to believe that the wall of separation can fall, and a brutal and bloody past be put to rest without ever firing even one weapon. However, there are enough historical examples to assure us this is entirely possible. I am providing you with an example most historians, regardless of politics, agree was one of the most successful strategies for large scale nonviolent peacemaking in written history. (There are also other excellent examples of nonviolent peacemaking provided to us by great leaders such as Ghandi and Martin Luther King, Jr.)

The largest and most recent example is that of the approach South Africa took when handling the ending of apartheid and the replacement of the existing government with a democratically elected government dedicated to ending racism and sexism. The apartheid government came into power in 1948. Descended from European ancestry, the rulers were a minority, outnumbered by the native population of ethnic African heritage. Afraid they could not hold their power, the ruling white minority began government-supported segregation in all areas of their community. Black citizens were often uprooted and many were sent to poverty-stricken resettlement camps. The whites ensured that they themselves would live in the best areas, with the best facilities and the best jobs. A great amount of violence occurred in South Africa for many years as the white minority was determined to hold onto its power.

In his book *No Future Without Forgiveness*, Archbishop Desmond Tutu explains how the falling of the Berlin Wall in late 1989 led to a moment in time that made the ending of apartheid possible. South Africa had been looked upon by the West as a stronghold against Communism. Therefore, Western nations allowed the system of apartheid to remain in place, unchallenged, until the end of the Cold War. With the threat of Communism gone, a new opportunity became available in South Africa to radically change the strict class system that had been built along racial lines. In this respect, one peaceful change led to another. On April 27, 1994, South Africa saw its first democratically elected government. President Nelson Mandela became the first democratically elected South African head of state.

With the election of a new government, the prevailing question was how to handle the past. Should there be a war tribunal, such as the one established in Nuremberg, Germany, after World War II to try war criminals? For a host of reasons, the new South African government felt this would not work for their country. They decided on an option that surprised many. They chose a system of amnesty and forgiveness for those who had persecuted and killed and maimed their fellow citizens in the name of apartheid. They didn't want blanket amnesty as they felt this would not allow an opportunity for people to tell their stories and heal the past. Therefore, Dullah Omar, the new Minister of Justice, introduced an act in Parliament to develop the Truth and Reconciliation Commission. President Nelson Mandela appointed Archbishop Desmond Tutu as its chairperson. Those who had committed crimes would be allowed to apply for amnesty, and come before the Truth and Reconciliation Commission, which would hear their case. The interim constitution, which allowed for the development of the Truth and Reconciliation Commission, said it best:

> This Constitution provides a historic bridge between the past of
> a deeply divided society characterized by strife, conflict, untold
> suffering and injustice and a future founded on the recognition of

human rights, democracy and peaceful co-existence and development opportunities for all South Africans, irrespective of color, race,
class, belief or sex. The pursuit of national unity, the well-being of
all South African citizens and peace require reconciliation between
the people of South Africa and the reconstruction of society . . .

Many people felt that justice was not rendered with the approach
used by the Truth and Reconciliation Commission. They could not
understand how people who had committed unbelievable atrocities
against others could be allowed to walk away with only a confession
of guilt, an acceptance of responsibility for what they had done and
a full disclosure of the facts. The perpetrators were not forced to
express remorse or even to apologize for their crimes, although many
of them chose to do so anyway.

When all conditions required by the Promotion of Unity and
Reconciliation Act were met, amnesty was granted immediately, and
the perpetrator's court record, related to that crime, became a blank
page. Both the perpetrator and the state were free from being held
accountable for the crime.

When explaining to people who questioned the Truth and Reconciliation Commission's understanding of justice, Reverend Tutu said:

One might go on to say that perhaps justice fails to be done
only if the concept we entertain of justice is retributive justice,
whose chief goal is to be punitive . . . we contend that there is
another kind of justice, restorative justice, which was character-
istic of traditional African jurisprudence. Here the central concern is not retribution or punishment. In the spirit of ubuntu,
the central concern is the healing of breaches, the redressing of
imbalances, the restoration of broken relationships, a seeking to
rehabilitate both the victim and the perpetrator . . . This is a far

more personal approach, regarding the offense as something that has happened to a person and whose consequence is a rupture in relationships. Thus we would claim that justice, restorative justice is being served when efforts are being made to work for healing, for forgiving, and for reconciliation.

As you can imagine, there was so much crying during the public confessions before the Truth and Reconciliation Commission that some people began to refer to them as the Kleenex Commission. The opportunity for confession and outpouring of emotion provided an opportunity for South Africa to heal the past, and begin a new and hopeful future. Forgiveness or reconciliation doesn't mean forgetting or condoning the atrocities committed: It means ending the cycle of violence.

While this story of nonviolent peacemaking is extraordinary, this doesn't mean that South Africa lived happily ever after without a worry or care. South Africans are still struggling and growing with their newfound freedom. The current leadership is ever reminded that above all they must not repeat the mistakes of the past.

Tomorrow's Peacemakers

Can today's youth generation give rise to the next Nelson Mandela or Desmond Tutu? Many would think not, believing that today's youth are too busy and distracted on their cell phones or with their iPods to really notice what's going on around them. But I disagree. I have a very different view of young people. They are activists, who are concerned about their government, health care, world peace, the environment and human rights. It's just that they connect to one another in a different manner.

Young people today live in a virtual world of instantaneous communication. Unlike youth of the '60s and '70s, today's young people don't have to gather in groups to connect unless they choose to. Take for example the youth revolution that led up to the 2008 U.S. presidential election. Large numbers of young people were on their cell phones, on the Internet, using instant messengers, using e-mail, blogs and social networking sites to support Barack Obama in an attempt to bring what they believed at the time would be sweeping changes to our country. Their revolution was more silent than the '60s, but my guess is that it will be just as profound. They didn't take to the streets, have sit-ins and demonstrations, but they *did* make their voices heard. They worked their electronic connections and engaged in the front lines of a community-organizing effort on a mass scale never before witnessed in this country. On the day of decision, the day of action, they joined with other generations and turned out in record numbers to vote for a new leader and what they believed would be a new direction for our country. There were no angry mobs, police barriers, tear gas or people being hauled off to jail. And yet, our young people played a very large role in massive social change as they voted for the first African-American man to become President of the United States of America.

Not all young people voted this way, and not everyone agrees with the choice of Barack Obama. That's perfectly okay. I am not advocating support for any particular political party or persuasion. The point I'm trying to make is that young people, having a variety of viewpoints, turned out in record numbers to make their voices heard and their will known because they wanted change. They didn't like what was going on in our country, but they didn't act out in anger or through violence. Their revolution was peaceful. To me, this shows that our young people are ready to embrace forgiveness and shows they would be very open to joining the Forgiveness Revolution, seeking new ways to make peace within our country and in our world.

Quantum Physics, Holograms—
Marvels of Modern Science—
Peacemaking and Forgiveness

In Chapter 3, we discussed how to move energy using the forgiveness technique to meet our personal dreams and goals. I explained how moving energy through our thoughts, prayers and meditations can be explained through quantum physics and the holographic universe. Universal laws can also be used to bring about world peace and reconciliation. The best news regarding the new and exciting methods is that you can wage a full campaign for world peace without leaving the comfort of your home. There are currently initiatives for peace that are scientifically proven to be effective. There is a movement called One % that may provide us with direction. One % is the first multi-method, multi-faith, whole community approach to peacemaking with prayer and meditation. Each person (based on their own faith tradition, or even if they have no particular faith tradition) is encouraged to meditate or pray for peace and happiness using the method with which they feel most comfortable.

This movement was organized to join diverse communities of all forms and faiths into the daily practice of prayer and meditation for peace and happiness and then to study the effect. The organization believes that when enough people meditate or pray deeply, there is a ripple effect of each individual's thoughts and goodwill, and that force spreads and touches the whole community. It also provides a good example for how to forgive a collective such as a government, nation, organization or institution.

This may sound flaky, but it is actually backed up by scientific research. Dr. John Davies, an internationally recognized expert in conflict management at the University of Maryland, has conducted tightly controlled critical research in war zones. His results were published in a professional peer-reviewed journal. Dr. Davies found that when just 1 percent of people in a community spend as little as twenty-five to forty-five minutes a day in prayer and meditation for peace, the whole community moves toward peace. His research found as much as an 80 percent decrease in violence within the community. He discovered that people not only tend to stop killing each other, but are able to come together and perceive new possibilities for cooperative work and partnership, even with their enemies.

This lets us begin to understand the tremendous effect that focused thought can have on the world. Prayer and meditation can work wonders individually—but who knew they could have such profound results when done in concert with others? Now, just imagine if 1 percent or more also focused on forgiveness as a technique for resolving conflicts between governments and nations. What if 1 percent of us focused our efforts on resolving conflicts governments have with their own people? What if people were taught to forgive the leaders of their own governments and those of other governments? Can you even begin to imagine the impact this would have in a very short time?

Methods used in the past to bring about forgiveness, reconciliation and peacemaking have given us a valuable road map. However, I believe peacemaking in the future will change with the times just like many things. It's important for us not to get so caught up in the past that we miss what is right in front of us. The Internet will afford new and more expanded opportunities for us to reach out to others from all over the world. It will allow us to organize great efforts to forgive, reconcile and make peace. In the future, prayer, meditation and directed thought will continue to be proven by science to soften the hearts and minds of those we're trying to reach. Now millions can do it virtually with just the click of a button.

Forgiveness: The Most Powerful Strategy

Forgiving doesn't mean forgetting or condoning. It doesn't mean becoming weak or not protecting our country when needed. Robin Casarjian, in her book *Forgiveness: A Bold Choice for a Peaceful Heart*, says:

> Until we learn to forgive—not condone, not turn our back on, not go numb on, not forget—but forgive, we will be run by our pain and anger. And, what's most insidious is that our anger will make attack appear reasonable and righteous. We will be in pain and project our pain outward. We will be the initiators of more pain, the perpetrators of more separation; more us and them; more subject and object. We will not learn the lessons that history has to teach.

Some may think forgiveness is a weak strategy compared with bullying nations into compliance with bombs and destruction. However, history teaches us over and again this kind of death and destruction serves no one. Maria Montessori, who founded the Montessori School, believed "Establishing lasting peace is the work of education."

Montessori recommends partnering with the scientific community to discover new strategies and techniques for achieving peace. She makes an interesting comparison of war to the bubonic plague, which is estimated to have taken the lives of one-third of Europe's population. She said that the plague was conquered only when its hidden causes became the object of scientific investigation. Like wars, epidemics of the plague broke out only sporadically and often unpredictably; were named for historical figures, like Pericles, Constantine and Gregory the Great; and often individuals were blamed and killed or groups of people were decimated. Montessori points out that it was scientific research that discovered the direct cause of the plague was a microorganism carried by fleas found on the large rat population that flourished in the unhygienic living conditions of the day. She said,

> "Without scientific methods of research, who could ever have found the direct causes of the plague?"

Applying scientific research to the forgiveness technique could lead to a whole new paradigm for creating and maintaining peace. Maybe one cause of war and unrest is lack of forgiveness for oneself and others. If proven true, scientific discovery would totally change the traditional methods that governments have used in the past to try to live in harmony with one another. It will become increasingly obvious that violence is not only counterproductive but completely unnecessary. *A new way,* one that not many people ever even considered, could emerge as the accepted strategy for maintaining peace and prosperity for all nations. What may have been considered weak because of its compassion and simplicity will be the strongest, wisest and most sought-after strategy of choice.

You may think this is silly, or an impossible concept—after all, people have been preaching forgiveness for years. The thing to remember is that a specific, simple technique for forgiving has never before been packaged in a form that is easy to teach, easy to understand, and works astonishingly well for many people who try it. Considering an age-old concept such as forgiveness in a totally new way may be the holy grail or "priceless pearl" we've been searching for.

Why Wage Peace Through Forgiveness Now?

For our young people, our old people, our divorced people, ourselves and anyone we care about, I believe the timing is perfect for bringing *The Law of Forgiveness* to the world. As demonstrated by the success of *The Secret*, the masses are beginning to become aware that there are universal laws and principles that can be tapped to better their existence. Also, the need to forgive and be forgiven is a universal theme that seems to resonate with everyone. If you ask people in a crowded room how many feel a need to forgive someone in their past or present, most often every hand is raised. It is rare that I meet someone who says they have worked through all of their forgiveness issues. Forgiveness has always been an important issue and is unlikely to go away. Why is the present the perfect time for the Forgiveness Revolution?

There exist many compelling reasons for "Why now?" All of the major news outlets keep repeating the theme that many Americans are hungry for change. Many Americans realize that the strategies of the past aren't working, and they are searching for new ways of being and interacting that will improve their own personal lives, as well as the lives of others who share their country and their world. I invite you to join the Forgiveness Revolution. This provides you with an exciting opportunity to join with others in a positive movement and participate in the tremendous results forgiveness can bring to our lives, our country and our world.

Why now? In addition to the tremendous results my clients have received from personal forgiveness, at this time in our history many Americans are searching for ways to develop better relationships internationally. Joining a positive movement such as the Forgiveness Revolution will offer structure and support for Americans to reach out to the international community in peace, repairing damaged relationships. Many Americans are considering war, and are concluding that war doesn't seem to be a good strategy for reaching a lasting peace. They are open to examining new methods for interacting with our world neighbors. The forgiveness affirmation technique that I teach is a perfect strategy to be considered, as it transcends all differences in ethnicity, religion, gender, culture and nationality. There is a word for forgiveness in every major language, demonstrating its cultural importance and universal appeal. All of the world's major religions and philosophies stress the need for forgiveness.

Why now? We have recently entered a new millennium. Prophets from several ancient cultures predicted the times in which we live would be pivotal—with a possibility of great peace, or an equal possibility of great destruction. Bringing *The Law of Forgiveness* and the Forgiveness Revolution to the world provides a rare opportunity for us to offer a powerful strategy that may actually assist with "fashioning the change" toward one of peace and reconciliation at this remarkable time in world history.

Believe it, because it's true: As a group of dedicated individuals intent on bringing a simple technique for forgiving and being forgiven to the world, we can actually provide powerful instruction that will assist with moving our country and our world toward an era of peace and reconciliation instead of one of destruction.

Forgive Locally, Reap the Benefits Globally

"And what do you think the earth will be like when the majority of men and women learn to be simple, and honest and true as

part of wisdom, and to work for Love and Beauty—the highest good?"

—Elbert Hubbard

In conclusion, it becomes obvious that the power of forgiveness is real whether it is enacted on a personal level between individuals, or on a more global level between nations. The type of forgiveness that is needed to achieve a lasting world peace can begin with a decision made by each individual to let go of his or her own personal grievances. First, we must forgive all the people we feel have wronged us. When we are able to let go of our own hurts and resentments, we enable others to do the same. This process is made a little easier now that we know that in return we shall certainly receive a blessing.

The greatest blessing will be achieved when the ripple of energy freed through each individual act of forgiveness combines to create a great groundswell the nations of the world can no longer ignore. On that day, without great fanfare, no rifle shots will be heard, walls of hatred and separation will fall and weaponry will be turned into plowshares, pruning hooks and artwork. The citizens of the world will be awestruck wondering how this peace could have been achieved so quietly. They will finally come to understand that true and lasting peace between nations can only manifest when their citizens forgive and make peace within themselves—this is what Jesus called the Kingdom Within. History has proven time and again that lasting peace cannot be achieved through wars and rumors of wars.

It is my sincere desire that all that has been learned about forgiveness through using the technique in this book can be directly applied to the broken relationships between the people and countries of our world and true healing can result, bringing in a new era of personal and global forgiveness, peace and reconciliation.

NOTES

Introduction

1   "The Law of Attraction is a Universal Law," Domino, Connie. *Law of Attraction: Develop Irresistible Attraction*. Raleigh: LOA Quantum Growth, 2007, 26.

3   "Pass an invisible boundary . . . " Thoreau, Henry David, *Walden, Or, Life in the Woods* (Boston: Ticknor and Fields, 1854), Chapter 18.

6   "Nature is the great giver . . . " Custer, Dan, *The Miracle of Mind Power* (New York: Prentice Hall Press, 1988), 75.

7   "They discovered that . . . " Racine, Ann, Joan Werner and Louis Racine. "Forgiveness with a Multicultural Emphasis." *Journal of Advanced Nursing*, 59 (3), 309.

8   "The very purpose of our life is to seek happiness . . . " The Dalai Lama, *The Art of Happiness* (New York: Penguin Putnam, Inc. 1998), 13.

9   "Forgive as the Lord . . . " Colossians 3:13, NIV.

9   "In forgiving others . . . " Skutch, Robert, *Journey Without Distance: The Story Behind A Course in Miracles* (Celestial Arts, 1984), 133–134.

12 "The Golden Rule . . . " Forgiveness and World Religions. http://wikipedia.org/wiki/forgiveness, October 24, 2007.

12 "The major religions . . . " Shared Belief in the Golden Rule: http://www.religious tolerance.org/reciproc.htm July 11, 2009.

13 "Therefore all things . . . " Matthew 7:12 KJV.

13 "Our Principles," Unitarian Universalist Association, at http://www.uua.org, July 09, 2009.

14 "Father, forgive them . . ." Luke 23:34, NLT.

15 "We are all made of energy . . . " Grabhorn, Lynn, *Excuse Me Your Life Is Waiting* (Hampton Roads Publishing Co., Inc., 2001), 13-14.

14 "I basically just talked to him . . ." "Ex-hostage: 'I wanted to gain his

trust,'" CNN News. See: http://www.cnn.com/2005/LAW/03/14/smith.transcript/index.html March 8, 2005.

Chapter 1

20   "The British military retaliated . . ." Bombing of Dresden Germany WWII. http://en.wikipedia.org/wiki/Bombing_of_Dresden_in_World_War_II, June 12, 2009.

21   "The Cross of Nails has become . . . " The Community of the Cross of Nails. See www.ccn-northamerica.org, www.crossofnails.org (accessed: October 29, 2007).

Chapter 2

38   "Forgiveness does not mean approval . . . " Hart, Louise, *The Winning Family: Increasing Self-Esteem in Your Children and Yourself* (Oakland, CA: Lifeskills Press, 1990), 39.

42   "The remarkable thing is . . . " Eric Hoffer as quoted in Hart, Louise, *The Winning Family: Increasing Self-Esteem in Your Children and Yourself* (Oakland, CA: Lifeskills Press, 1990), 17.

46   "Here is a forgiveness technique . . . " Ponder, Catherine, *The Dynamic Laws of Prosperity.* (DeVorss Publications, 1996), 46–47.

Chapter 3

49   "He describes in his book . . . " Luskin, Fred, *Forgive for Good: A Proven Prescription for Health and Happiness* (San Francisco: Harper Collins, 2002), xv–xvii.

49   "Luskin also writes about . . . " Luskin, Fred, *Forgive for Good: A Proven Prescription for Health and Happiness* (San Francisco: Harper Collins, 2002), 80.

49   "Until recently . . . " Worthington, Everett, Jr., Campaign for Forgiveness Research, www.forgiving.org, 2007.

50   "Dr. Worthington . . . " Wax, Heather, What is Forgiveness Worth? Science and Spirit, May/June, 2004, 34.

51   "It would be madness to jeopardize . . . " Wax, Heather, "What is Forgiveness Worth?" *Science and Spirit,* May/June, 2004, 34.

54   "Dr. Dossey also describes . . . " Dossey, Larry, *Healing Words: The Power of Prayer and the Practice of Medicine* (San Francisco: Harper Collins, 1993), 180.

54   "The universally connected hologram . . . " Braden, Gregg, *The Divine*

Matrix: Bridging Time, Space, Miracles, and Belief (Carlsbad, CA: Hay House, 2007), 108.

55   "Is it possible to live . . . " Braden, Gregg, *The Divine Matrix: Bridging Time, Space, Miracles, and Belief* (Carlsbad, CA: Hay House, 2007), 106.

55   "We live in a nonlocal world . . . " Russell Targ as quoted in Braden, Gregg, *The Divine Matrix: Bridging Time, Space, Miracles, and Belief* (Carlsbad, CA: Hay House, 2007), 106.

57   "If I have seen further than others . . . " Newton, Isaac. See http://en .wikipedia.org/wiki/Isaac_Newton October 24, 2007.

Chapter 5

87   "The most accepted model . . . " Kübler-Ross, Elisabeth, *On Death and Dying* (New York: Touchstone, 1969).

87   "Support groups provide . . . " Grosskopf, Barry, *Forgive Your Parents, Heal Yourself*, (New York: The Free Press, 1999), 64.

88   "One of my favorite . . . " Bloomfield, Harold, Melba Colgrove, and Peter McWilliams, *How to Survive the Loss of a Love* (Mary Books Prelude Press, 2000).

88   "In nature, loss . . . " Bloomfield, Harold, Melba Colgrove and Peter McWilliams, *How to Survive the Loss of a Love* (Mary Books Prelude Press, 2000), 2.

95   ". . . beneath anger lies . . . " Zukav, Gary, and Linda Francis, *Heart of the Soul: Emotional Awareness* (New York: Simon and Schuster, Inc., 2001), 132–133.

95   "Rage is an excruciating . . . " Zukav, Gary, and Linda Francis, *Heart of the Soul: Emotional Awareness* (New York: Simon and Schuster, Inc., 2001), 134.

96   "When someone is exceptionally angry . . . " Enright, Robert, *Forgiveness Is a Choice: Step by Step Process for Resolving Anger and Restoring Hope* (American Psychological Association, 2001), 62–63.

98   "Ninety percent of healing . . . " Tipping, Colin C., *Radical Forgiveness: Making Room for the Miracle*, 2nd ed. (Marietta, GA: Global 13 Publications, 2002), 25.

98   "He believes that if we learn . . . " Tipping, Colin C., *Radical Forgiveness: Making Room for the Miracle*, 2nd ed. (Marietta, GA: Global 13 Publications, 2002), 253–290.

Chapter 7

119   "Therefore I tell you . . . " Mark 11:24, NIV.

120   "I went to all the life centers . . . " Myrtle Fillmore quoted in Witherspoon, Thomas E., *Myrtle Fillmore: Mother of Unity* (Unity Books, 2000), 42–43.

120   "Around 1888, two years . . . " Witherspoon, Thomas E., *Myrtle Fillmore: Mother of Unity* (Unity Books, 2000), 43.

Chapter 8

132   "This hierarchy was a model . . . " Maslow's Hierarchy of Needs. See http://en.wikipedia.org/wiki/Maslow's_hierarchy_of_needs, October 24, 2007.

137   "When forgiveness arrived at . . . " Kraybill, Donald, Steven Holt, and David Weaver-Zercher, *Amish Grace* (Hoboken, NJ: John Wiley Sons, Inc., 2007), 52.

138   "Forgive us our debts . . . " Matthew 6:12, NKJV.

138   "In a world where faith . . . " Kraybill, Donald, Steven Holt, and David Weaver-Zercher, *Amish Grace* (Hoboken, NJ: John Wiley Sons, Inc., 2007),183.

141   "The psychological hold . . . " Sawyer, Jeffrey, "America, Mexico, and Beyond," *The Sun*, June 2004. See http://d20608.u48.plankdesign.com/_media/article/pdf/342_Sawyer.pdf.

Chapter 9

144   "Forgiveness and reconciliation . . . " Desmond Tutu as quoted by Campaign for Forgiveness Research. See www.forgiving.org, October 24, 2007.

145   "A fundamental change . . . " *Merriam-Webster's Collegiate Dictionary*, 10th ed. (Springfield, MA: Merriam Webster, Inc., 2001).

146   "The way we see the world . . . " Covey, Stephen, *The 7 Habits of Highly Effective People* (New York: Simon and Schuster, 1989), 23.

148   "Some people may find . . . " 2006 Fact Sheet on Mortality: Adolescents and Young Adults. National Health Adolescent Health Information Center.

149   "More African-American men . . . " Wilson, Basil, "Blacks, The College Campus and Prison" in *Carib News,* The New York Community Media Alliance Edition 189, October 2005. See http://www.indypressny.org/nycma/voices/189/editorials/editorials/

151 "In his book . . . " Tutu, Desmond, *No Future Without Forgiveness* (New York: Doubleday, 1999), 3.

152 "This Constitution provides . . . " Tutu, Desmond, *No Future Without Forgiveness* (New York: Doubleday, 1999), 45–46.

153 "One might go on to say . . . " Tutu, Desmond, *No Future Without Forgiveness* (New York: Doubleday, 1999), 54–55.

154 "As you can imagine . . . " Tutu, Desmond, *No Future Without Forgiveness* (New York: Doubleday, 1999), 163.

156 "There is a movement . ." One %. See www.whenonepercent.org, October 24, 2007.

158 "Until we learn . . . " Casarjian, Robin, *Forgiveness: A Bold Choice for a Peaceful Heart* (Bantam Books, 1992), 216.

158 "Establishing lasting peace . . . " Montessori, Maria, *Education and Peace* (Oxford, England: Clio Press, 1992), 9.

161 "And what do you think the world will be like . . . " Hubbard, Elbert. *The Philosophy of Elbert Hubbard*. East Aurora, NY: The Roycrofters, 1916, 64.

BIBLIOGRAPHY

"2006 Fact Sheet on Mortality: Adolescents and Young Adults." National Health Adolescent Health Information Center.

Bloomfield, Harold, Melba Colgrove and Peter McWilliams. *How to Survive the Loss of a Love*. Los Angeles: Mary Books Prelude Press, 2000.

Braden, Gregg, *The Divine Matrix: Bridging Time, Space, Miracles, and Belief*. Carlsbad, CA: Hay House, 2007.

Casarjian, Robin. *Forgiveness: A Bold Choice for a Peaceful Heart*. Bantam Books, 1992.

Covey, Stephen. *The 7 Habits of Highly Effective People*, New York: Simon and Schuster, 1989.

Custer, Dan. *The Miracle of Mind Power*. New York: Prentice Hall Press, 1988.

Desmond Tutu as quoted by Campaign for Forgiveness Research, http://www .forgiving.org/, October 24, 2007.

Domino, Connie. *Law of Attraction: Develop Irresistible Attraction*. Raleigh, NC: LOA Quantum Growth, 2007.

Dossey, Larry. *Healing Words: The Power of Prayer and the Practice of Medicine*. San Francisco: Harper Collins, 1993.

Elisabeth Kübler-Ross. Model: The Five Stages of Grief. http://en.wikipedia.org .wiki/Five_Stages_of_Grief, October 24, 2007.

Enright, Robert. *Forgiveness Is a Choice: Step by Step Process for Resolving Anger and Restoring Hope*. American Psychological Association, 2001.

Eric Hoffer as quoted in Hart, Louise. *The Winning Family: Increasing Self-Esteem In Your Children and Yourself*. Oakland, CA: Lifeskills Press, 1990.

Ex-hostage: "I wanted to gain his trust." *CNN News*. http://www.cnn.com/2005/ LAW/03/14/smith.transcript/, March 8, 2005.

Forgiveness and World Religions. http://wikipedia.org/wiki/forgiveness, October 24, 2007.

Grosskopf, Barry. *Forgive Your Parents, Heal Yourself.* New York: The Free Press, 1999, 64.

Hart, Louise. *The Winning Family: Increasing Self-Esteem in Your Children and Yourself.* Oakland, CA: Lifeskills Press, 1990, 39.

Hubbard, Elbert. *The Philosophy of Elbert Hubbard.* East Aurora, NY: The Roycrofters, 1916, 64.

Isaac Newton. http://en.wikipedia.org/wiki/Isaac_Newton October 24, 2007.

Kraybill, Donald, Steven Holt and David Weaver-Zercher. *Amish Grace.* Hoboken, NJ: John Wiley & Sons, Inc., 2007.

Luskin, Fred. *Forgive for Good: A Proven Prescription for Health and Happiness.* San Francisco: Harper Collins, 2002.

Maslow's Hierarchy of Needs. http://en.wikipedia.org/wiki/Maslow's_hierarchy_of_needs, October 24, 2007.

Matthew 7:12, KJV.

Merriam-Webster's Collegiate Dictionary, 10th ed. Springfield, MA: Merriam Webster, Inc., 2001.

Montessori, Maria. *Education and Peace.* Oxford, England: Clio Press, 1992.

One %. www.whenonepercent.org, October 24, 2007.

"Our Principles," Unitarian Universalist Association, at http://www.uua.org, June 9, 2009.

Ponder, Catherine. *The Dynamic Laws of Prosperity.* DeVorss Publications, 1996.

Racine, Ann, Joan Werner and Louis Racine. "Forgiveness with a Multicultural Emphasis." *Journal of Advanced Nursing,* 59 (3), 309.

Russell Targ as quoted in Braden, Gregg. *The Divine Matrix: Bridging Time, Space, Miracles, and Belief.* Carlsbad, CA: Hay House, 2007, 106.

Sawyer, Jeffrey. "America, Mexico, and Beyond." *The Sun,* June 2004, http://www.thesunmagazine.org/_media/article/pdf/342_Sawyer.pdf.

Schell, Jonathan. *The Unconquerable World: Power, Nonviolence, and the Will of the People.* New York: Metropolitan Books, 2003.

Shared Belief in the Golden Rule: http://www.religioustolerance.org/reciproc.htm. July 11, 2009.

Skutch, Robert. *Journey Without Distance: The Story Behind A Course in Miracles.* California: Celestial Arts, 1984.

The Community of the Cross of Nails. http://ccn-northamerica.org, http://crossofnails.org, October 29, 2007.

Thoreau, Henry David, *Walden, Or, Life in the Woods* (Boston: Ticknor and Fields, 1854).

Tipping, Colin C. *Radical Forgiveness: Making Room for the Miracle,* 2nd ed. Marietta, GA: Global 13 Publications, 2002.

Tutu, Desmond. *No Future Without Forgiveness.* New York: Doubleday, 1999.

Vanzant, Iyanla. *One Day My Soul Just Opened Up.* New York: Simon and Schuster, 1998.

Wax, Heather. "What Is Forgiveness Worth?" *Science and Spirit,* May/June, 2004, 34.

Wilson, Basil; *Blacks, The College Campus and Prison,* The New York Media Alliance, Carib News. Edition 189, October 2005. http://www.indypressny.org/nycma/voices/189/editorials/editorials/ June 22, 2009.

Witherspoon, Thomas E. *Myrtle Fillmore: Mother of Unity.* Unity Village, MO: Unity Books, 2000.

Worthington, Everett, Jr., Campaign for Forgiveness Research, www.forgiving.org, 2007.

Zukav, Gary. *Thoughts from the Seat of the Soul.* New York: Simon and Schuster, Inc., 1994.

ABOUT THE AUTHOR

Connie Domino, B.S.N., M.P.H., R.N., is a nationally acclaimed life coach, and author of the inspirational book *Law of Attraction: Develop Irresistible Attraction*. Connie has been teaching Law of Attraction workshops since 2001. She is known for the success of her clients who consistently report manifesting dreams and goals quickly from her clear, easy-to-understand and powerful instruction. She is also a trainer, speaker, public health educator and registered nurse. She has more than twenty years of experience in business, health promotion and wellness education. She also has training and experience as a support group facilitator, educational counselor and motivational speaker. She is an assistant clinical professor in Nursing at the University of North Carolina at Chapel Hill. Connie has been interviewed on local and national radio and television talk shows. She received her bachelor of science degree in Nursing from Florida State University, and her master's degree in Public Health from the University of North Carolina at Chapel Hill. Connie lives in Raleigh, North Carolina, with her husband and two children.

For more information about books, CDs, newsletters, life or organizational coaching, workshops, and/or consultation calls, please visit Connie's websites at:

www.TheLawofForgiveness.com
www.JoinTheForgivenessRevolution.com
www.conniedomino.com